Hiking The Grand Canyon And Havasupai

Headwaters of the Thunder River literally flow out of the cliffs

Hiking The Grand Canyon And Havasupai

Larry A. Morris

AZTEX Corporation, Tucson AZ

Photo Credits

William Epling, Jr.
Brenda Morris
Larry A. Morris
Kathy Perino
Nicholas J. Vitale

Cover and book design: Yoka Schaufelberger

Typesetting: Maria L. Montijo

Printing and binding: Fairfield Graphics,
Fairfield, Penn

ISBN 0-89404-053-7

Library of Congress Catalog Card No. 81-68384

Printed in the United States of America

AZTEX Corporation
P O Box 50046, Tucson, AZ 85703

Contents

This book is dedicated to:
Bren
Sue, Bev, Jackie, Jan, Kim
Greg
and to Galen, who started it all.

Introduction

The Grand Canyon. There are few places on earth that offer such an awesome display of nature's artwork. The sight of this timeless wonder jolts the senses. People scurry about the edge looking for the one spot, the correct angle, the proper lighting in order to snap the one photograph which will capture it all. It is an impossible task. There is too much to it—and it changes: Sometimes sleepy and misty in the early morning, bold and daring in the blazing noonday sun, brooding and contemplative at evening-time. And the night fills with mystery. From the edge, the Canyon beckons softly for you to enter, but it also emits an ominous warning not to enter as an ill-prepared unbeliever. The Canyon can be both seductive and unforgiving.

As you pull the Canyon around you, it awakens ancient memories of gods at war and play. Long repressed feelings from our primordial wellspring begin to stir and you realize that the Canyon is not just a monument carved from stone and seen through the magic of reflected light. The Canyon is much more personal, it becomes part of you and you it until the two spirits join with mutual understanding and respect. Living here is not just stone but the entire spectrum of human emotions.

It is my hope that this book will dissuade you from entering the Grand Canyon as an ill-prepared unbeliever, but, will assist you in taking the steps necessary to plan and have an informative, enjoyable and safe Grand Canyon hiking experience. The information contained herein is a blend of information gained through the author's nearly fifteen years of Grand Canyon hiking experiences; extensive research of historical, geological, and hiking literature; and discussions with other experienced Grand Canyon hikers including National Park Service personnel. The book is designed to present as much information as possible without becoming lengthy or cumbersome.

While the information in this book was current at the time of writing, conditions at and policies about the Grand Canyon change frequently. As you begin to plan your trip, you are encouraged to contact Grand Canyon National Park or Havasupai Tourist Enterprise personnel to receive any new details which may affect your trip. As an example, last Fall initial plans for a trip from the North to the South Rim had to be changed because of an earlier than expected closing of the North Rim Entrance Road for paving. Park Service and Havasupai personnel have always been friendly, cooperative and most helpful in planning trips. On a day-by-day basis, they are your best resources.

As one view, one hike, one photograph, or one paragraph cannot begin to capture all that is the Grand Canyon, one book, including this one, cannot capture and transmit the totality of the Grand Canyon experience. It is strongly suggested that you give the Recommended Reading section of this book careful consideration. Four authors should top your list: Harvey Butchart, probably the only person who has ventured into just about every nook and cranny of the Grand Canyon; Colin Fletcher, the only person known to have walked the entire length of the Grand Canyon; Stephen Hirst, who has written a compelling history of the Havasupai Indians; and J. Donald Hughes, who has compiled an excellent portrayal of man's history in the Grand Canyon.

Read on, prepare carefully, and enjoy your Grand Canyon experience.

Mule Train

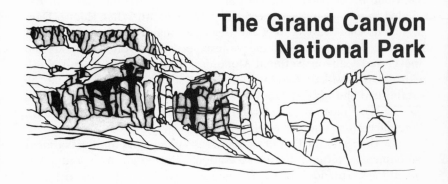

Chapter 1

The Grand Canyon National Park

The Grand Canyon National Park is located in the northwestern corner of the State of Arizona. It begins below Vermilion and Echo Cliffs near the mouth of the Paria River and extends along the Colorado River for nearly 277 miles (446 kilometers) to Grand Wash Cliffs near Arizona's western boundary. With the exception of Indian Reservation land, the Park includes all of the interior of the Grand Canyon and some sections of the adjoining plateaus, an area encompassing 1,892 square miles (4,900 square kilometers). The Grand Canyon National Park is administered by the National Park Service, U.S. Department of the Interior.

Before the present boundaries of the Grand Canyon National Park were established in 1975, various sections of the Grand Canyon had come under a variety of governmental jurisdictions. The Grand Cañon Forest Reserve was established by President Benjamin Harrison in 1893 and in 1897 the Reserve was placed under the jurisdiction of the General Land Office, Department of the Interior. In 1906, a Grand Canyon Game Reserve was established to protect "game" animals in the Grand Canyon area but not their natural predators.

In 1907, the Division of Forestry was completely reorganized resulting in the creation of the Grand Canyon National Forest. Using the 1906 Act for the Preservation of American Antiquities, President Theodore Roosevelt established the Grand Canyon National Monument in 1908. By so doing, the Grand Canyon National Forest was divided into three sections: The Grand Canyon National Monument, the Kaibab National Forest and the Coconino National Forest. All three remained under the management of the National Forest Service.

In 1916, the National Park Service was created and on February 26, 1919, President Woodrow Wilson established the Grand Canyon National Park. The Park was only about one-half the size of the current Park and covered only the central section of the Grand Canyon. Excluded were most of the eastern and western areas. When Hoover Dam was completed in 1936, the Lake Mead National Recreational Area was established which included the western part of the Grand Canyon from the Grand Canyon National Monument (not Park) to Grand Wash Cliffs. On President Lyndon Johnson's last day in office in 1969, he established the Marble Canyon National Monument thus protecting the eastern part of the Grand Canyon from the National Park boundary upstream to the Paria River.

By the 1970s the Grand Canyon was a patchwork quilt of National Monuments, National Forests, a National Recreation Area and a National Park. In addition, the Navajo, Hualapai and Havasupai Reservations also included parts of the Grand Canyon area.

For years various conservation groups, governmental agencies and the U.S. Congress saw the need to unify the protection of the Grand Canyon by incorporating as much of it as possible in an expanded National Park. But expansion became problematic because there were those who wanted to build more dams in the area and the Indian tribes had legitimate claims to portions of the Canyon. The controversy raged on for several years but a plan was finally worked out: no dams would be built in the Grand Canyon, the Havasupai Indians would receive an expanded reservation, and the Grand Canyon National Park could still be expanded. On January 3, 1975, President Gerald R. Ford signed into law the Grand Canyon Enlargement Act bringing, exclusive of Indian reservation land, the former Grand Canyon and Marble Canyon National Monuments and part of the Lake Mead National Recreational Area east of Grand Wash Cliffs into the Grand Canyon National Park. Further expansion of the Park to include additional plateau lands may be possible in the future.

Chapter 2

The Colorado River And The Grand Canyon

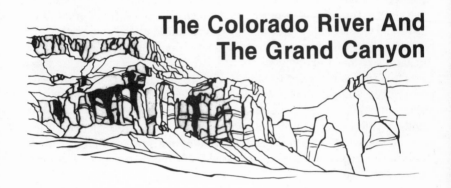

The Colorado River begins in the Rocky Mountain National Park in north-central Colorado and flows southwestward in a meandering fashion until it empties into the Gulf of California in Mexico, a distance of approximately 1,440 miles (2,317 kilometers). Among 135 rivers in the United States with a length of over 100 miles (161 kilometers), the Colorado River ranks a respectable sixth. Although the Colorado River flows through other beautiful wilderness areas and deep canyons, the 277 miles (446 kilometers) through the Grand Canyon are the most spectacular and breathtaking.

In 1776, Father Francisco Garcés, a Jesuit priest who traveled from present day Tucson, Arizona, to the Colorado River and then northward along the Colorado to what is now called the Grand Canyon, named the reddish-brown silt-laden river "Rio Colorado," (Red River). However, the name "Colorado" was not made official until 1921 when the U.S. Congress assigned the name to the entire length of the river.

With the advent of modern man's increasing need for electrical energy and his ability to harness natural resources through dams, the Colorado River is seldom *colorado* these days. Indeed, once one of the most silt-laden waterways in the United States, most of the silt is now trapped behind the Glen Canyon Dam a few miles upstream from the Grand Canyon National Park. The Glen Canyon Dam was completed in 1963 despite the vociferous protests of conservationist groups and individuals all over the United States and some foreign countries.

When Major John Wesley Powell and his nine intrepid adventurers set out to explore the uncharted Colorado River in 1869, he wrote fondly of the beautiful glens, magnificent arches and grottos and other marvelous formations he found in Glen Canyon. He also described a chamber carved from the rock nearly 200 feet (61 meters) high, 200 feet (61 meters) wide, and 500 feet (152 meters) long which seemed to enhance the sounds of music. He named this beautiful chamber the "Music Temple." Sadly, Powell's beloved music chamber and the rest of Glen Canyon's beauty are now flooded by a huge reservoir which bears his name, Lake Powell.

Before Glen Canyon Dam was constructed, the Colorado River would rise and fall depending upon the climatological changes in the Colorado River Basin. The rate of flow ranged from about .5 to 100 million gallons per minute (about 2 to 375 million liters per minute). Now between about 3 and 7 million gallons per minute (about 11 to 26 million liters per minute) are released from the dam depending upon the demand for electricity.

Lee's Ferry, some .3 of a mile (.48 kilometers) above the Paria River, is the point (Mile 0) from which mileage in the Grand Canyon is measured. From Lee's Ferry to the Grand Wash Cliffs, the Colorado River drops nearly 2,215 feet (675 meters), an average of somewhat less than 8 feet per mile (1.5 meters per kilometer) or twenty-five times greater than the "mighty" Mississippi River. The average depth of the Colorado River is 50 feet (15 meters) with the deepest spot, 110 feet (34 meters), located at Mile 114.3. The river's width varies from between 200 to 300 feet (61 meters to 91 meters) and travels at an average of 20 to 25 miles per hour (32 to 40 kilometers per hour). During floods, the Colorado River still unleashes its awesome power and forces rocks and

boulders to crash into each other as they are moved downstream. The resultant sound and ground vibrations can be rather frightening to the unwary hiker. Swimming in the Colorado at any time is very risky business—do not attempt it.

The average depth of the Grand Canyon is 1 mile (1.6 kilometers), while the average width from rim to rim is about 10 miles (16 kilometers). The North Rim is about 1,000 feet (305 meters) higher than the South Rim, a fact to keep in mind if you plan a rim-to-rim hiking trip.

The Colorado River

Length:	About 1,440 miles (2,317 kilometers) of which 277 miles (446 kilometers) are in the Grand Canyon National Park.
Width:	Average is about 300 feet (91 meters).
Depth:	Average is about 50 feet (15 meters).
Descent:	In the Grand Canyon National Park, the river drops 2,215 feet (675 meters) for an average of about 8 feet per mile (1.5 meters per kilometer).
Rapids:	Nearly 70 major rapids in the Grand Canyon.
Velocity:	Average in the Grand Canyon is about 20—25 miles per hour (32—40 kilometers per hour) with strong undercurrents.
Temperature:	Average is about 45^{0}F (7^{0}C).

The Grand Canyon

Length:	277 miles (446 kilometers).
Width:	600 feet (183 meters) to 18 miles (30 kilometers). Average is about 10 miles (16 kilometers)
Depth:	Average is about 1 mile (1.6 kilometers). From North Rim: 5,700 feet (1,737 meters). From South Rim: 4,500 feet (1,372 meters).
Elevations:	North Rim Ranges: 8,000 to 9,000 feet (2,438 to 2,743 meters). South Rim Ranges: 6,000 to 7,000 feet (1,828 to 2,134 meters). Canyon Floor: About 2,400 feet (732 meters.)

Colorado River

Chapter 3

A Geological Time Machine

The Grand Canyon is one of the few places on earth where you will have the opportunity to walk through nearly two billion years of the earth's five billion years of geological history. Some familiarity with the major geological formations found in the Grand Canyon can assist you when hiking the wilderness trails. This information should also help make any Grand Canyon hiking experience more meaningful.

Kaibab Limestone And Toroweap Formation

These upper two layers of limestone are very similar and form the rim of the Canyon. These formations are deposits from when the Grand Canyon region was twice covered by seas during the Permian Period (about 200 to 250 million years ago). The colors are predominately gray and red-buff.

Coconino Sandstone

When the Grand Canyon area was a desert, winds blowing predominately from the north created sand dunes from 300 to 500 feet (91 to 152 meters) thick. The sand is now fossilized with the grains held together by calcite. The sandstone's color is light tan or buff.

17

Hermit Shale

Beneath the light tan or buff of the Coconino Sandstone, you will find a reddish formation with an approximate thickness of 300 feet (91 meters). This is the Hermit Formation consisting of shales, siltstones and mudstones.

Supai Group

Blending with the red of the Hermit Shale is the Supai Group consisting of four red-colored formations with an approximate thickness of 900 feet (274 meters). The Supai Formation contains sandstones, shales, siltstones, and limestones and is generally harder than the Hermit Formation. Both formations provide evidence of fresh water deposits and shifting flood plain activity.

Redwall Limestone

One of the most prominent features in the Grand Canyon is the Redwall Limestone Formation. It is approximately 500 feet (152 meters) thick and although its true color is gray limestone, it has actually been stained red by the Supai and Hermit Formations located just above it. The Redwall Limestone Formation contains evidence that the Grand Canyon area was covered by at least three seas.

Devonian Temple Butte Limestone

More of this formation can be seen in the western part of the Canyon than in the eastern part where most of it has eroded away. Yet another sea was responsible for this formation. The color is purple to pinkish gray.

Muav Limestone

An unconformity exists between the Temple Butte Formation and the Muav Limestone Formation. The former is dated in the late Devonian Period while the latter is of Cambrian age (formed by the shallow Cambrian Sea). Ninety-five to 115 million years of Paleozoic deposits have apparently eroded away. The Muav Limestone is yellowish gray or buff colored. It is about 35 feet (11 meters) thick in the eastern part of the Grand Canyon with the thickness increasing to about 600 feet (183 meters) in the western part at the base of Toroweap Valley.

Bright Angel Shale

Also formed by deposits from the Cambrian Sea, this grayish-green shale averages about 400 feet (122 meters) thick. The Tonto Plateau was formed by the easily eroded Bright Angel Shale.

Tapeats Sandstone

Another sedimentary deposition of the Cambrian Sea, this formation is about 200 to 300 feet (61 to 91 meters) thick. It is predominately brown in color and forms the rim of the Inner Gorge.

Inner Gorge

The Inner Gorge consists of Bass Limestone and the oldest exposed rocks in the Grand Canyon. The limestone is gray. Also look for dark gray schists and gneisses often intruded with white or pink granite. You have just stepped back in time about two billion years.

Note the strata on the far ridge—Thunder River area.

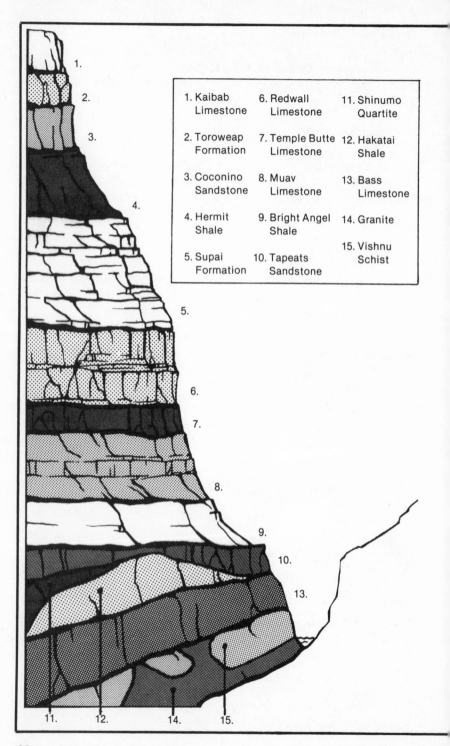

1. Kaibab Limestone

2. Toroweap Formation

3. Coconino Sandstone

4. Hermit Shale

5. Supai Formation

6. Redwall Limestone

7. Temple Butte Limestone

8. Muav Limestone

9. Bright Angel Shale

10. Tapeats Sandstone

11. Shinumo Quartite

12. Hakatai Shale

13. Bass Limestone

14. Granite

15. Vishnu Schist

A Geogical Time Machine

Predominant Land Form	Approximate Thickness Exposed Feet	Meters	Predominant Color	Approximate Age in Millions of Years	Period	Era
1. Cliff	300	91	Light Gray	250	Permian	
2. Cliff	250	76	Red Buff	255	Permian	
3. Cliff	350	107	Light Tan or Buff	260	Permian	
4. Steep Slope	225	69	Red	265	Permian	
5. Slopes with Ledges	900	274	Red and Gray	285	Permian and Pennsylvanian	
6. Cliff with Ledge	500	152	Gray Stained Red	335	Mississippian	Paleozoic
7. Cliff	100	30	Purplish	355	Devonian	
8. Slopes Ledges Cliffs	35 to 600	11 to 183	Yellowish Gray	515	Cambrian	
9. Bench	350 to 600	107 to 183	Greenish Gray	530	Cambrian	
10. Cliff	225	69	Brown	545	Cambrian	
13. Slope	200	61	Gray	1,200	Pre Cambrian	Late
15. Steep Slope	Unknown		Dark Gray intruded with Pink or white	2,000	Pre Cambrian	Early

Scale 1" = Approx. 828.23529 feet
▬▬▬▬▬▬ = Approx. 1, 000 feet

Inner Gorge and Colorado River

Chapter 4

Climate

The temperature and weather conditions at the Grand Canyon vary not only with the seasons but also with the area. For example, the South Rim is generally drier and hotter than the North Rim while the Inner Gorge is hotter and drier than both.

South Rim

The average maximum and minimum temperatures on the South Rim are 62 °F (17 °C) and 35 °F (2 °C) respectively.

Spring (March—May)

An excellent time of year to hike the Grand Canyon from the South Rim. The weather is usually delightfully warm, sunny and dry. But the nights can be cold with temperatures usually dropping into the 30s F (−1° to 4 °C). Spring weather is also somewhat unpredictable so be prepared for a sudden downward shift in temperature and possible rain-showers.

Summer (June—August)

During the summer months the temperature on the South Rim usually ranges from a high in the 80s F (high 20s C) to a low around 50°F (10°C). June is the driest month, while July and August are the wettest with afternoon thunderstorms a rather common occurrence.

Fall (September—November)

Fall is another delightful time to hike the South Rim trails. Daytime temperatures are usually in the 50s to 70s F (10 to 20s C) while the nighttime temperatures are usually in the 30s to 40s F (−1° to 9°C). Like spring, the fall is normally warm and sunny, but colder weather and rainshowers can happen suddenly.

Winter (December—February)

The winters on the South Rim are relatively mild with the high temperatures usually in the 40s F (4 to 10°C) and the low temperatures around 20°F (−7°C). The upper parts of the trails are often covered with snow and ice, but as you descend, the trails normally become clear.

North Rim

The average maximum and minimum temperatures on the North Rim are 56°F (13°C) and 30°F (−1°C) respectively.

Open Season (May—September)

Due to an average yearly snowfall of about 5 feet (1.5 meters), the North Rim is normally closed from early October to early May. During the open season, the high temperatures are usually in the 60s to 70s F (15 to 20s C) and the low temperatures are usually in the 30s to 40s F (−1° to 9°C). Because of the mild temperatures, camping on the North Rim can be most pleasant; however, most North Rim trails face the south resulting in high temperatures. June is the driest month, while August usually brings the most rainfall.

Inner Gorge

The Inner Gorge has a desert climate with high temperatures and little rainfall. To avoid the very high summer temperatures, the best months to hike into the Inner Gorge are late March through early May, plus October and November. During these months the high temperatures are usually in the 70s to 80s F (20s to 30s C) and the low temperatures are usually in the 40s to 60s F (4 to 20s C). Also during these months you normally will not have to contend with snow on the South Rim.

During the summer, temperatures in the Grand Canyon often exceed 100°F (38°C) with temperatures around 115°F (46°C) not that uncommon. June is usually the driest month and August the wettest.

In the winter, snow rarely reaches the Canyon floor and the precipitation is usually less than 1 inch (.03 meter) each month. The temperatures are usually in the 50s to 60s F (10 to 20s C) during the day and the 30s to 40s F (−1° to 9°C) at night.

North Rim

Celsius And Centimeters

Month	South Rim			North Rim			Inner Gorge		
	Max	Min	Precip	Max	Min	Precip	Max	Min	Precip
January	5	−8	3.35	3	−9	8.05	13	2	1.73
February	7	−6	3.94	4	−8	8.18	17	6	1.91
March	11	−4	3.50	7	−6	6.68	22	9	2.01
April	16	0	2.36	12	−2	4.39	28	13	1.19
May	21	4	1.68	17	1	2.97	33	17	.91
June	27	8	1.07	23	4	2.18	38	22	.76
July	29	12	4.60	25	8	4.90	41	26	2.13
August	28	12	5.72	24	7	7.24	39	24	3.56
September	24	8	3.96	21	4	5.05	36	21	2.56
October	18	2	2.79	15	−1	3.51	29	14	1.65
November	11	−3	2.39	8	−4	3.76	20	8	1.09
December	6	−7	4.11	4	−7	7.19	14	3	2.21

Source: Grand Canyon Climates, GRCA 0—24, 11-17-77 Revised, National Park Service, Grand Canyon National Park, Grand Canyon, Arizona 86023.

Average Temperatures And Precipitation

Fahrenheit And Inches

Month	South Rim			North Rim			Inner Gorge		
	Max	Min	Precip	Max	Min	Precip	Max	Min	Precip
January	41	18	1.32	37	16	3.17	56	36	.68
February	45	21	1.55	39	18	3.22	62	42	.75
March	51	25	1.38	44	21	2.63	71	48	.79
April	60	32	.93	53	29	1.73	82	56	.47
May	70	39	.66	62	34	1.17	92	63	.36
June	81	47	.42	73	40	.86	101	72	.30
July	84	54	1.81	77	46	1.93	106	78	.84
August	82	53	2.25	75	45	2.85	103	75	1.40
September	76	47	1.56	69	39	1.99	97	69	.97
October	65	36	1.10	59	31	1.38	84	58	.65
November	52	27	.94	46	24	1.48	68	46	.43
December	43	20	1.62	40	20	2.83	57	37	.87

Desert area near Thunder River

Chapter 5

Preparation and Information

A. Equipment

In order to make your Grand Canyon trip an enjoyable and safe one, select your equipment carefully. Although each hiker has his/her own equipment preferences and needs, the following information is presented to assist in selecting equipment appropriate for hiking in the Grand Canyon.

Footwear

One of the most important pieces of equipment you should have is a pair of properly-fitted boots designed specifically for hiking and/or climbing. Do not hike in street shoes, tennis or jogging shoes, thongs or boots with smooth soles. Even on maintained trails, the footing can be unsure. A pair of boots with soles made for gripping can help prevent a dangerous fall. In the summer the ground temperature is often well over 125° F (52°C) so it is very important to have footwear designed to protect your feet from the heat. Do not hike in new boots. Make sure you have your boots broken-in before you begin your hike.

Experienced hikers often wear at least two pairs of socks while hiking. The inner sock should be light- to medium-weight and capable of absorbing moisture from the feet. The second sock should be heavier to provide extra padding around the foot and ankle. Always carry extra socks and bootlaces.

29

To help prevent blisters, "second-skin" products like Moleskin can be applied directly to the feet covering areas where you anticipate a blister might form. Moleskin and similiar products consist of a soft but very durable material with an adhesive backing. They normally are available in sheets allowing you to cut any shape or size to fit your particular need. Remember, apply Moleskin *before* you begin your hike in order to help *prevent* blisters.

Clothing

In the summer you should wear clothing that will protect you from the sun but also allows your body to breathe properly. A long-sleeved shirt, long pants, and a hat are recommended. In the winter, you may need the extra protection of gloves, a down vest or jacket, and long underwear.

Rain Gear

Whether you are backpacking or day hiking, it is always a good idea to carry some kind of rain gear. Usually, a rain poncho of good quality will do the job. To avoid the problem of condensation, select a poncho that is water repellant but also allows moisture from the body to evaporate.

Backpacks

For overnight excursions, select a backpack large enough to hold everything you are going to need to get you in and out of the Canyon safely. In selecting a backpack make sure it is good quality. Both the frame and the pack should be light but strong. A waistband is an attractive feature because it helps distribute the weight more evenly between the shoulders and hips. You may also want to have a water-proof cover for your pack and sleeping gear. Make sure the frame fits you properly and is comfortable. For day hikes, you may only need a comfortable rucksack (no frame) large enough to carry your food and other gear.

Sleeping Gear

During the summer, a lightweight sleeping bag or even a lightweight blanket will normally suffice. At other times, you may be more comfortable in a somewhat heavier bag, especially if you camp at higher elevations. Although some hikers prefer the comfort of an air mattress, a foam pad is usually more convenient and dependable. Self-inflating foam pads are now available which combine the convenience of foam with the extra support of air. Air pillows are also available but many hikers prefer to make a pillow from extra clothing.

Tent

Depending upon how much comfort you require while hiking, you may or may not want to carry a tent. Rainstorms in the Canyon are not uncommon and you can expect some snow at the higher elevations during the winter. If you prefer to protect yourself from the elements, you may want to carry a lightweight but strong backpacking tent complete with floor and rainfly. You might also consider a less expensive plastic tube tent; however, tube tents are subject to condensation and do not offer the same overall comfort and protection as a tent designed for backpacking.

Cooking Stove

Campfires are *prohibited* below the rims of the Grand Canyon so you will need another source of heat to cook your food. Many types of portable backpacking stoves are available. Select one that is lightweight, compact, easy to light and produces heat efficiently. The two most popular types are the gasoline and butane models. Both are compact and produce heat efficiently. Your choice may depend upon your own personal desires. Some major points of comparison (and debate) follow: gasoline stoves usually require some fiddling before they will light, while most butane stoves require only that you touch a flame to them and you are ready to go. However, some butane models flame-out frequently and require relighting. Extra fuel for gasoline stoves must be carried in and transferred from a separate container to the stove, a minor inconvenience unless you are prone to spilling. Some fuel bottles have been known to leak, a major inconvenience in any event and especially so around smokers. A new butane cartridge connects to most models without much fuss and seldom leaks. As you use the gasoline fuel, your load becomes lighter but an empty butane cartridge weighs nearly the same as a full one. (Of course you will pack the empty cartridge out of the Canyon and *not* leave it there.) Overall, the gasoline stove probably creates more noise than does the butane stove. Take your choice.

Cooking And Eating Utensils

There are those who feel a camping experience is not complete without the smell of fresh eggs and bacon cooking in a cast-iron skillet and black coffee brewing in an old-time chuckwagon pot. If you are unable to part with this bit of nostalgia, you are better off to camp in your own backyard or neighborhood park rather then carry the excess weight in and *out* of the Canyon. Keep it simple and lightweight. For cooking, seldom will you need more than a couple of different sized lightweight pots for boiling water, a lightweight skillet for heating or frying some foods, and a handle to lift the utensils from the fire. For eating your gourmet's delight, you can usually make do with a lightweight plate, a knife, fork and spoon set, and a cup. Some prefer the legendary "Sierra Club cup" made of stainless-steel, while others prefer the more "homey" look and feel of plastic. Lightweight cooking utensils come in many forms. The most convenient are those that nest together to reduce the bulk.

Containers For Water

Containers for water come in a variety of shapes and sizes. Depending upon the length of your trip and the availability of water along the route you should select the size and types to fit your needs. The most popular for short trips are the quart size aluminum or plastic canteens. Some have the added convenience of clips used to fasten the canteen to your belt. The wide mouth plastic bottles are carried in the pack but are very convenient if you plan to add a powdered substance such as lemonade or Gatorade. The collapsible plastic container with a sturdy handle and a pouring spout is most handy around a campsite. Much less desirable but observed being carried by some misguided souls are used plastic bleach bottles, glass soft drink bottles (one in each hand), and large metal canteens with a wide strap and covered with fake fur, swinging like a pendulum from the hiker's neck.

Food

As you can imagine, the choice of food is a very personal thing. Some hikers feel they are being cheated of a true wilderness experience if they do not fuss about the campsite for hours mixing this and that and creating everything from bran muffins to Hungarian goulash. Sometimes the eating ritual becomes more important than the actual hiking experience. Others survive on sandwiches and fresh fruit. For the most part, your selection of food should depend upon your need for ritual and the length of your trip. If you are hiking just for the day, the weight of the food becomes less critical than if you were going on a five-day excursion. At any rate, try to keep it simple and lightweight.

While most dried foods may not receive a five-star rating for taste, they certainly receive high ratings for convenience and lack of weight and bulk. Dried food comes in many forms and can be found in grocery and backpacking stores. Most require only the addition of boiling water to a pouch containing the food. This makes the after-meal clean-up a very simple matter. Believe-it-or-not, freeze dried lasagne supplemented with a little fresh fruit at the end of a long day's hike can satisfy all but the most discerning palate. In case of an emergency, it is always wise to carry extra food.

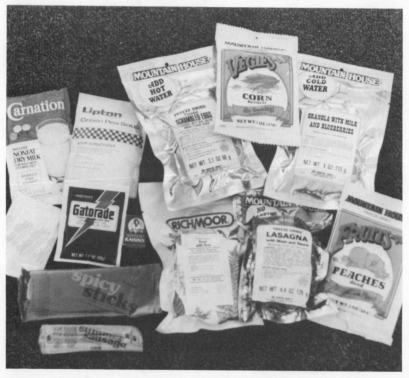

Topographic Maps And Compass

Topographic maps and an accurate compass are essential for hiking the wilderness trails. Of course, just having a compass and the maps will not help if you don't know how to use them. Your local hiking clubs or backpacking equipment store should be able to provide assistance in compass and map reading. Several U.S. Geological Survey topographic maps of the Grand Canyon are presented in this book. These maps may be purchased at local backpacking equipment stores or map centers. If unavailable locally, maps can be ordered by mail from the U.S. Geological Survey or the Grand Canyon Natural History Association. Topographic maps are also available at the Visitors Center on the South Rim and at the Grand Canyon Lodge on the North Rim.

For an Index to Topographic Maps of Arizona (includes the Grand Canyon) write:

> Branch of Distribution
> U.S. Geological Survey
> Box 25286
> Federal Center
> Denver, Colorado 80225

For a list of topographical or other Grand Canyon maps write:

> Grand Canyon Natural History Association
> Post Office Box 399
> Grand Canyon, Arizona 86023

Flashlight

You should carry a lightweight flashlight with fresh batteries or energy cells. Extra batteries and a spare bulb are also recommended.

Signal Mirror And Whistle

In case of an emergency, it is a good idea to have a signal mirror or reflector and a whistle. Flashing light and the shrill sound of a whistle will carry much farther than the frantic calls of an injured hiker.

Snake Bite Kit

Although bites from poisonous snakes are not commonplace in the Grand Canyon, rattlesnakes do live in some parts of the Canyon. Snake bite kits can also be used for spider bites and scorpion stings. Make sure you know how to use your kit *before* you need it. Rattlesnakes, spiders, and scorpions usually do not wait around for people to read instructions before they bite.

First Aid Kit

You can purchase backpacking first aid kits or you can develop one to fit your own needs. Whichever one you choose, it should be complete enough to administer aid in all common emergencies such as cuts, bruises, sprains and eye injuries. At the very least, your first aid kit should contain the following:

> Adhesive tape (a roll of 1 or 2 inch width)
> Antiseptic
> Aspirin
> Band-aids (have several of the various shapes and sizes)
> Butterfly band aids
> First-aid cream
> Gauze bandage and/or pads (a roll of the 2 inch width
>   and/or 2 to 4 inch square pads)
> Moleskin
> Needle
> Salt Tablets
> Razor blade (single edge type)

Other Important Items

Other items you should carry are candles, sun screen, knife, tweezers, scissors, clipper, chapstick, insect repellant, butane lighter, matches in a waterproof container, extra pins for backpack and frame, and water purification tablets. Since most of the vegetation in the Grand Canyon does not work at all well as toilet tissue, it would be wise to have in your possession the ubiquitous partial roll of toilet paper (scented and/or flowered only if you insist).

A typical campsite

B. Physical Conditioning

It has been said that Grand Canyon hiking is the reverse of mountain hiking in that the climb occurs at the end of the hike when you are likely to be the most fatigued rather than at the beginning when you are rested and raring to get on the trail. Keep this fact in mind as you begin to get yourself into condition for your Grand Canyon trip. That is, condition yourself for overall stamina and endurance plus make sure you increase the strength of your legs sufficiently to propel (drag?) yourself onward and upward, always upward, at the end.

How to get into condition? The answer to this question rests with your overall physical and medical condition. If you do not already know what shape you are in, it is probably time for a physical examination and some medical advice. If you get winded walking from the refrigerator to the television set, you may be a superb candidate for a bad case of the Grand Canyon cardiacs and will require much more work to get into shape than someone who traverses the same route with élan.

Some achieve physical fitness by engaging in all sorts of strenuous physical activities—running, swimming, racquetball, weight-lifting, shopping, calisthenics, football, soccer, *ad infinitum*. However, helpful these activities may be, the best way to prepare yourself for hiking is to *hike*. To prepare for the Grand Canyon select areas near you which require a lot of steep incline hiking. If you are trapped in the city, find a tall building with lots of stairs and *start hiking*. To see if you are ready for hiking out of the Grand Canyon, load your pack with about 30 or 40 pounds (14 or 18 kilograms), strap it on your back and hike up several flights of stairs. If you soon find yourself wishing you had taken the elevator, you are not ready yet. However, keep at it and eventually you should be able to build the strength and stamina necessary to get you in and out of the Canyon safely. Otherwise, it may be prudent to carry an extra supply of BenGay or money to pay for the mule or helicopter sent to get you out.

C. Water

Although some of the maintained trails may have water available, the water situation in the Grand Canyon can be summarized in two words: *seasonal* and *unreliable*. With the exception of the Colorado River, many trails have no reliable water sources at all and others with seemingly reliable sources may suddenly become dry. To be safe, purify all water taken from springs, streams, creeks, and even the Colorado River. *Always check with the Backcountry Office for the latest information about the availability of water before you begin your hike.*

As a general rule, you should carry at least two quarts or two liters of water per person per day if some water is available on the trail. If you anticipate having difficulty in finding water, you should consider carrying twice this amount. In any case, always carry extra water just to be safe.

D. Wilderness Roads

Access to many of the trailheads requires traveling over several miles of roads used infrequently. Many of these roads are not maintained on any regular basis and often become quite difficult to traverse. In inclement weather most are not passable at all. Use extreme caution when traveling these roads. Although passenger cars have survived trips on some of these roads, it is far better to use a vehicle with a high road clearance and even a four-wheel drive. Carry extra fuel, water and food in case of an emergency. Always check with the U.S. Forest Service or the National Park Service on the condition of these roads before you begin your trip. For your safety, you are also required to give an expected time of return and to check in when you complete your trip.

E. Cairns

Some of the wilderness trails may have cairns marking the trailhead and parts of the route. Although a welcome sight after some time searching for the proper route, cairns in the Grand Canyon are not always a reliable source of direction. Sometimes cairns are built by someone more lost than you and never destroyed once the error was discovered. When encountering cairns it is always advisable to check

with your maps and look for other signs of a trail before proceeding. If you anticipate finding a cairn at a particular spot and do not, you may not necessarily be lost. Often, cairns are destroyed by flash floods and rock slides. Here your map, a compass and experience are your best guides. The point of all this is: while cairns can be helpful, do not rely too heavily on them to find your way but be prepared to find the route through other means.

F. Sanitation

For your convenience and for the protection of the ecosystem, many campgrounds come complete with toilet facilities. However, most wilderness areas are not so blessed and you will have to become more resourceful (or become adept at holding it for a few days). Good wilderness sanitation practices are quite simple. Select a site at least 300 to 400 feet (91 to 122 meters) from a watersource of any kind, dig out a hole about 6 to 8 inches (15 to 20 centimeters) deep, while preserving the sod, if any, completely fill in after, and replace the sod. Simple. One problem is what to do with the used toilet paper. Some hikers prefer to bury it with the waste but paper takes longer to decompose than human waste and may be dug up and scattered by critters (especially if you insisted on carrying the scented kind). It is far better to place the used paper in a plastic bag and pack it out with the rest of the trash. The same is true of tampons and sanitary napkins, a favorite target for critters. Also, as a common courtesy try not to select a spot which would make a lovely (unless you ruin it) campsite for your fellow hikers.

G. Trash

Several years ago someone (who will remain nameless) strongly advocated designating the Grand Canyon as the nation's sanitary landfill. After all, he reasoned, the hole was already there and how easy it would be just to drop the garbage in. And, it would take years to fill. Further, he continued to reason, no one needs a big hole in the ground—so why not use it for something really practical? Although this rather inane idea was taken seriously by only a few equally inane individuals, the basic concept that the Grand Canyon is a big place and can tolerate a lot of trash persists even today.

The idea was wrong then and it is wrong now. The ecosystem in the Grand Canyon is very fragile and the continued accumulation of man's discardables can only produce more destruction. Further, campsites and trails cluttered with all sorts of trash certainly detract from the esthetic quality of the grandeur about you. Please do not deceive yourself, your little bit of trash, *no matter what it is*, does matter. Plan carefully so you will not have a lot of heavy trash, pack an extra plastic bag large enough to hold it, and pack it out. Leave not a trace of your visit. PACK IT ALL OUT.

Havasu Falls

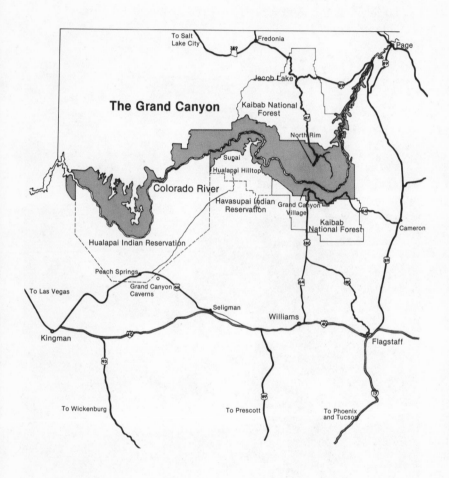

The Grand Canyon

Colorado River

To Salt Lake City

Fredonia

Page

Jacob Lake

Kaibab National Forest

North Rim

Supai

Hualapai Hilltop

Havasupai Indian Reservation

Grand Canyon Village

Kaibab National Forest

Cameron

Hualapai Indian Reservation

Peach Springs

To Las Vegas

Grand Canyon Caverns

Seligman

Williams

Kingman

Flagstaff

To Wickenburg

To Prescott

To Phoenix and Tucson

Chapter 6

The South Rim

General Information

The Grand Canyon Village inside the park offers food, lodging, camping, service stations, post office, banking, medical services, groceries, backpacking equipment, showers, laundry, pet kennels and other related services. To reduce traffic congestion, the Canyon Shuttle offers free transportation between several scenic spots along the rim and the village area. Although the South Rim is open on a year-round basis, not all of the facilities are open during the winter. To reach the developed area of the North Rim from the Grand Canyon Village by automobile requires traveling a distance of about 214 miles (344 kilometers).

There are two entrances to the South Rim of the Grand Canyon National Park:

South Entrance Station

Located on U.S. 180 and Arizona 64 approximately 80 miles (129 kilometers) northwest of Flagstaff and approximately 60 miles (97 kilometers) north of Williams. Flagstaff and Williams are located on I-40 (U.S. 66).

East Entrance Station (Desert View)

Located on Arizona 64 approximately 32 miles (51 kilometers) west of Cameron, Arizona. Cameron is located on U.S. 89 on the Navajo Indian Reservation.

Food And Lodging Inside The Park

The Grand Canyon National Park is under the jurisdiction of the National Park Service; however, all accommodations on the South Rim, except for trailers and camping, are operated by a private company, Grand Canyon National Park Lodges. Even so, all prices for accommodations, meals and other services within the park must be approved by the Park Superintendent. A list of approved prices can be obtained from the restaurants and lodges.

The Grand Canyon National Park is under the jurisdiction of the National Park Service; however, all accommodations on the South Rim, except for trailers and camping, are operated by a private company, Grand Canyon National Park Lodges. Even so, all prices for accommodations, meals and other services within the Park must be approved by the Park Superintendent. A list of approved prices can be obtained from the restaurants and lodges.

While most inside the park lodges are located on or near the rim, only a few rooms in the El Tovar Hotel provide a view of the Canyon. It is advisable to make reservations for lodging several months in advance, especially for the summer season. To make reservations for lodging inside the park call (602) 638-2401 or (602) 638-2631.

El Tovar Hotel

This rustic hotel was built near the rim in 1904 of rough-hewn pine logs and native stone. One of the original Fred Harvey hotels, it is considered a Grand Canyon historic landmark and is listed on the National Register for Historic Places. Gourmet dining is a tradition in the El Tovar Dining Room and Lounge.

Bright Angel Lodge

This stone and log lodge was designed by Mary Jane Colter and is considered by some as her masterpiece. She also designed the Desert View Watchtower and the Phantom Ranch. One of its outstanding features is a fireplace built with rocks from the different Grand Canyon strata placed in their proper geological sequence. The Bright Angel Lodge is near the rim and features both room and cabin accommodations plus a family restaurant, lounge, snack bar and coffee shop.

Thunderbird And Kachina Lodges

These two modern facilities are located between the El Tovar Hotel and the Bright Angel Lodge. Both offer deluxe rooms and suites.

Yavapai Lodge

In a wooded setting near the Visitor Center, the Yavapai Lodge is a modern lodge motel facility with a snack bar. The Yavapai Cafeteria, Yavapai Fast Food, and Yavapai Lounge are nearby. The lounge provides nightly entertainment during the summer.

Grand Canyon Motor Lodge

This motor lodge facility provides motel rooms and cabins at rates generally lower than the other facilities in the park. It also features a cafeteria.

Motor Lodge Mushwhip Unit

Named for the Hopi Kachina who is the guardian of the Grand Canyon, this is the newest addition to the Motor Lodge facility. It features one or two floor units with several rooms equipped for the handicapped.

Babbit's General Store And Delicatessen

No lodging is available at Babbit's General Store but it does offer a delicatessen, complete grocery supplies, backpacking and camping equipment.

Backpacking Equipment Rental

During the summer months, backpacking equipment can be rented from Grand Canyon Trail Guides located in the old Santa Fe Railroad Depot in Grand Canyon Village.

Food And Lodging Outside The Park (Tusayan Area)

Moqui Lodge

Of the three full service motels located near the park's South Entrance, the Moqui Lodge is nearest to the entrance. It provides motel rooms, tennis courts, riding stables, a restaurant and lounge. (602) 638-2424.

Red Feather Motel

Modern motel rooms and a restaurant can be found at this 110-room motel. (602) 638-2673.

Canyon Squire Resort Hotel

This large facility is located nearest to the Grand Canyon Airport. It features modern rooms, tennis, bowling, swimming, a restaurant and lounge. (602) 638-2681.

Camping Inside The Park

To obtain up-to-date information regarding the reservation system currently in use for campsites, contact:

> Grand Canyon National Park
> P. O. Box 129
> Grand Canyon, Arizona 86023

Mather Campground

Located near the Visitor's Center, Mather Campground has over 300 campsites. Restrooms and water are available within the campground. Located nearby is a Camper Service Building which provides showers and laundry facilities. Reservations are required.

Trailer Village

Located next to Mather Campground, this facility has nearly 200 spaces with electricity, water and sewer hook-ups. Reservations are required.

Desert View Campground

This campground is located about 20 miles (32 kilometers) east of the Grand Canyon Village on the East Rim Drive. It has facilities for camping plus recreational vehicles. Usually operates on a first-come first-served basis.

Camping Outside The Park (Tusayan Area)

Ten X Campground

This campground, operated by the U.S. Forest Service, is located about 10 miles (16 kilometers) south of Grand Canyon Village. Although water is usually available, there are no hook-ups of any kind.

Grand Canyon Camper Village

This is a privately-operated facility providing about 250 spaces with hook-ups. Also available are a general store and a fast food restaurant. (602) 638-2887.

Inner Canyon Trails And Camping

Reservations And General Information

In order to protect the Inner Canyon from damage due to over use, the National Park Service has placed a limit on the number of overnight campers. It is necessary, therefore, to plan your trip well in advance and then make reservations with the Backcountry Reservation Office. Currently, reservations are accepted three months in advance and even then you may have difficulty, especially during the summer. It is a good policy to have two or three alternative trips planned in case you cannot get reservations for your first choice. In most cases, camp-sites may not be occupied for more than one or two nights per trip. For your own safety and for the protection of the environment, camp only in designated campgrounds and wilderness camping areas. Failure to obtain a permit can result in a costly fine and/or a jail sentence.

Since hiking conditions in the Grand Canyon often change quickly and dramatically, Park Service policies regarding hiking and camping often change in response. To obtain up-to-date information about reservations and hiking conditions contact:

Backcountry Reservations Office
Box 129
Grand Canyon National Park
Grand Canyon, Arizona 86023
(602) 638-2474

The South Rim area has three maintained trails: Bright Angel, Kaibab, and River. All other South Rim trails, called "wilderness trails," are not maintained and range from good to bad condition. Most wilderness trails are old mining trails that have been abandoned for over fifty years. Rock slides, erosion and natural vegatation have taken their toll. Since the wilderness trails can be hazardous, it is strongly recommended that you gain Grand Canyon hiking experience on the maintained trails before attempting a wilderness trail. If you are not an experienced backpacker, you may not be issued a permit to hike the wilderness trails.

North Kaibab Trail going up Bright Angel Canyon

Bright Angel Trail on South Rim

Maintained Trails

Bright Angel Trail

Taking advantage of a natural break in the Canyon's cliffs created when the Bright Angel Fault lifted the strata westward, prehistoric Indians found their way and established a narrow foot trail to a veritable oasis nearly half-way into the Canyon. This oasis, now called Indian Gardens, was used by prehistoric and Havasupai Indians to cultivate crops.

The trail developed by the Indians was used by miners in the late 1800s. Pete Berry, Niles and Ralph Cameron widened the trail in 1890—91. Although they improved the trail for mining purposes, they soon discovered that more money could be made from tourism than mining. In 1903, Ralph Cameron bought out his two partners and soon gained sole control of the trail by filing mining claims at most of the scenic points in the area. At one time, his claims totaled more than 13,000 acres (5,261 hectares) of vintage Grand Canyon! In control of the trail and the most desirable spots at the Canyon, Ralph Cameron operated the trail as a toll road charging each person desiring to descend into the Canyon, one dollar.

Cameron was not without his troubles, however. The Santa Fe Railway had brought rail service to the Canyon in 1901 and, of course, was very interested in breaking Cameron's strong grip on the tourist trade. Santa Fe challenged Cameron's mining claims in court and after a long legal battle the claims were finally declared invalid in 1920.

In the meantime, Coconino County took over the toll rights in 1912. By 1928, the county decided it needed an access road to the Canyon from Williams, Arizona more than it needed a toll trail and an exchange with the National Park Service was worked out. Utilizing the Civilian Conservation Corps, the National Park Service had the lower section of the trail leading to the Colorado River improved during the 1930s. The National Park Service has since made other improvements.

Located near the head of Bright Angel Trail is Kolb Studio. The Kolb brothers, Ellsworth and Emery, came to the Grand Canyon in 1902. After working at various jobs around the area, they began a rather profitable business of taking photographs of tourists starting their mule rides down Bright Angel Trail. The Kolb brothers also explored and photographed areas of the Grand Canyon others had not yet entered including Cheyava Falls in Clear Creek Canyon during 1908. Their most notable feat, however, occurred from September, 1911, to January, 1912, when they became the first to make a Powell-like expedition by boat down the Colorado River while recording their experiences on motion picture film.

Bright Angel Trail is 7.8 miles (12.6 kilometers) long from the trailhead to the Colorado River and River Trail. The trail consists mostly of a series of steep switchbacks descending the Bright Angel Fault to Indian Gardens and then steeper switchbacks generally following Pipe and Garden Creeks to the Colorado River. A few less steep and generally straight areas exist near and on either side of Indian Gardens. The trail is usually maintained in very good condition and open year-round, although the top section of the trail may experience some snow in the winter. During the summer, the mid-day heat can be extreme, so it is best to hike during the early morning or late afternoon. Today, Bright Angel Trail is the most heavily traveled of all the Grand Canyon trails. If you are looking for solitude, you will not find it here. Instead, you will find a rather steady parade of tourists from around the world—mule-trains, hikers and backpackers. Even so, the Bright Angel trip can still be an enjoyable one.

A short distance from the trailhead you will pass through the first of two man-made tunnels. At one time Indian pictographs could be seen in this area but now most have been destroyed by vandals. The second tunnel stands at the edge of the Bright Angel Fault. If you look to the west you can see that the rocks are about 190 feet (58 meters) higher than those to the east. The fault switchbacks begin here.

Mile-and-a-Half Resthouse (1.6 miles; 2.6 kilometers) and Three Mile Resthouse (3.1 miles; 5.0 kilometers)—Two resthouses where you can find shade, an emergency telephone and water (May through September only).

Jacob's Ladder—Just below Three Mile Resthouse is a set of steep switchbacks known as Jacob's Ladder. The "Ladder" descends the Redwall Formation using a break in the sheer cliff caused by the Bright Angel Fault.

Indian Gardens (4.5 miles; 7.2 kilometers)—You have now descended about 3,100 feet (940 meters) below the rim. Indian Gardens offers water, camping, resthouses, tables and a ranger station all nestled beneath towering cottonwood trees first planted by Ralph Cameron in the 1900s.

Plateau Point—At Indian Gardens you will find a side trail leading across the Tonto Plateau to Plateau Point. The trail is delightfully flat and only 1.5 miles (2.4 kilometers) one way. At Plateau Point you will be nearly two-thirds of the way into the Canyon. The scenery is marvelous, and you can look straight down to the Colorado River rushing along nearly 1,300 feet (395 m) below you.

Garden Creek—For about 1.2 miles (2 kilometers) below Indian Gardens, the trail follows fairly near Garden Creek.

Although the water looks and sounds inviting, DO NOT DRINK IT because it is contaminated by the corral and leach field at Indian Gardens.

The Devil's Corkscrew—As the trail leaves the Garden Creek area you will encounter a very steep set of switchbacks, aptly named The Devil's Corkscrew. Once below the "Corkscrew" the trail generally follows Pipe Creek for about 0.9 mile (1.5 kilometers) to the Colorado River and River Trail. Pipe Creek, like Garden Creek is contaminated so DO NOT DRINK THE WATER.

The River Resthouse—At the junction of Bright Angel and River Trails you will find a resthouse with an emergency telephone *but no water*. A chemical toilet is also in the area.

Devil's Corkscrew

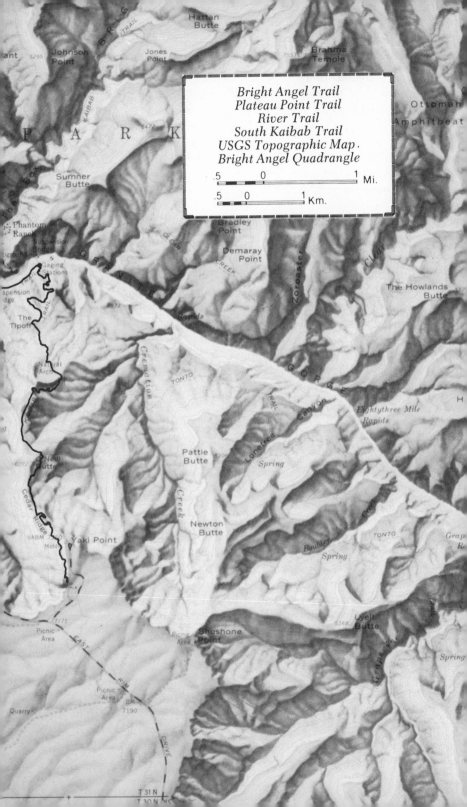

Bright Angel Trail
Plateau Point Trail
River Trail
South Kaibab Trail
USGS Topographic Map
Bright Angel Quadrangle

.5   0   1 Mi.

.5   0   1 Km.

The River Trail

Constructed in 1936 by the Civilian Conservation Corps, River Trail provides the shortest (1.7 miles; 2.7 kilometers) connection between Bright Angel Trail and South Kaibab Trail. River Trail is relatively level and generally follows the Colorado River above the south bank. This trail provides an excellent view of the Colorado River and the vishnu schist walls of the Inner Gorge. You will also travel across a mini sand dune. Expect very high temperatures in this entire area during the summer.

Bright Angel Campground

To reach Bright Angel Campground from the Bright Angel Trail direction, follow the River Trail upstream (easterly) until you come to the first of two suspension bridges spanning the Colorado River. This bridge, known as the Silver Bridge, was built in the late 1960s primarily to support a cross-canyon pipeline which carries water from Roaring Springs, located near the North Rim, to the Canyon floor, across the Colorado River, and up to the South Rim. Silver Bridge also provides access to Bright Angel Campground and the Phantom Ranch area. As you cross the Silver Bridge, you can see the pipeline supported beneath. Once across the Silver Bridge you will pass by a mule corral, the River Ranger Station and then you will find the campgrounds along the west bank of the Bright Angel Creek.

Phantom Ranch

Between 1903—07, "Uncle Dee" Woolley and his son-in-law, David Rust, constructed a trail from the North Rim to the Colorado River, across the river by cable-car, and up to Indian Gardens. The trail became known as the Old Kaibab Trail or Cable Trail and was used until the River Trail was completed in the 1930s.

During the construction of the Cable Trail, a camp for the construction workers was established along the east bank of Bright Angel Creek near the Colorado River. The camp was also used by David Rust as a resting point for his guided tours. The camp became known as Rust's Camp until 1913 when it was renamed Roosevelt's Camp because Theodore Roosevelt made a stop there.

In order to provide overnight accommodations for the tourists using the very popular mule-trips to the bottom of the Grand Canyon, Fred Harvey used the site of the old Rust-Roosevelt Camp to build the Phantom Ranch in 1922. Phantom Ranch was designed by Mary Jane Colter who also designed the Desert View Watchtower, Bright Angel Lodge, Lookout Studio, and Hermit's Rest. Accommodations at the Phantom Ranch included a large dining room and tourist cabins. At one time a swimming pool was provided.

Presently, the Phantom Ranch provides meals, cabins, and dormitory accommodations. Used primarily by mule-riding tourists, reservations are necessary:

Reservations Department
Grand Canyon National Park Lodges
Grand Canyon, Arizona 86023
Telephone: (602) 638-2401

When the dining hall is closed, hikers can find refreshments at the snack bar on the north side of the hall.

The Phantom Ranch area is located at the base of North Kaibab Trail about .25 mile (.40 kilometer) north of the Bright Angel Campground and about .75 mile (1.2 kilometers) north of the Colorado River and Kaibab Bridge.

*Phantom Ranch sign reads: Phantom Ranch
Dining Hall
Meals by reservation only*

South Kaibab Trail

In 1924, the National Park Service began construction on the Kaibab Trail in order to provide visitors with an inner-canyon, toll-free trail. At that time the Bright Angel was still a toll trail. It took nearly four years to complete the cross-canyon South and North Rim Kaibab Trails. The effort certainly was not wasted because the South Kaibab Trail, which generally follows ridges instead of side canyons, offers the most spectacular views of the Grand Canyon.

To reach the trailhead, take the East Rim Drive to Yaki Point Road. Follow the Yaki Point Road for only about 0.3 mile (0.5 kilometer) then follow the road to your left into a parking lot. The trailhead is just north of the parking lot.

South Kaibab Trail is the steepest rim-to-river trail and no water is available until you reach Bright Angel Campground near the Colorado River. During the summer, you can expect very little shade and high temperatures along most of the trail plus very high temperatures at the lower elevations. Ascending this trail from the river during the summer is most unwise.

Although South Kaibab Trail is fairly well traveled, it does not have as much traffic as Bright Angel Trail. You will encounter mule-trains, however. The distance to the Colorado River is 6.3 miles (10.1 kilometers). Some of the landmarks you will see along this trail are presented below:

> *Cedar Ridge*—The Kaibab Trail descends quickly, nearly 1,500 feet (450 meters) from the Rim to Cedar Ridge in just 1.5 miles (2.4 kilometers). Cedar Ridge provides very good views in general and an excellent view of O'Neill Butte in particular. You can also look below and see the Tonto Plateau and part of the Tonto Trail. For those in need, chemical toilets are located at Cedar Ridge.
>
> O'Neill Butte is the red Supai Sandstone formation just to the north of and nearly level with Cedar Ridge. It was named for William Owen "Buckey" O'Neill, an Arizona Territory prospector, businessman, author, judge, reporter and sheriff. He was also the mayor of Prescott in the 1890s. "Buckey" O'Neill was killed in the charge up San Juan Hill with Roosevelt's Rough Riders.

Skeleton Point—As you descend below Cedar Ridge to Skeleton Point, the grade is somewhat more gradual and there are fewer switchbacks. The unhurried hiker will be rewarded with spectacular views. At Skeleton Point, it is time to tighten your boots because the gradual descent gives way to a series of very steep switchbacks. The views continue to be excellent as the trail descends the Redwall and then moves across the Tonto Plateau.

Tonto Trail Junction—Tonto Trail and South Kaibab Trail cross at about 4.4 miles (7.1 kilometers) from the South Kaibab Trailhead. Just a short distance north of this junction on the Kaibab Trail, you will find chemical toilets and an emergency telephone. Turning to the left (southwest) on Tonto Trail will bring you to Indian Gardens, a distance of 4.6 miles (7.4 kilometers).

Panorama Point—Your first really good view of the Colorado River, the Bright Angel Campgrounds, and the Phantom Ranch area begins at Panorama Point which is located at a little over 0.5 mile (0.8 kilometer) from the Tonto Trail Junction. This is an excellent place to pause for awhile and simply enjoy. A set of steep switchbacks descending down the Inner Gorge begins here.

South Kaibab Trail near Panorana Point

River Trail Junction—Just before reaching the Colorado River, the trail meets River Trail. At this junction, a distance from the South Rim of about 6.0 miles (9.7 kilometers), River Trail follows the south bank of the Colorado River downstream for about 1.7 miles (2.7 kilometers) connecting with Bright Angel Trail. For more information about River Trail, see page 56.

Tunnel, Kaibab Bridge and the Colorado River—About .25 mile (.40 kilometer) below the River Trail Junction you will pass through a tunnel blasted from solid rock. On the other side of the tunnel you will find a suspension bridge spanning the Colorado River. This bridge, known as the Kaibab Bridge, was built in 1928 to complete the rim-to-rim route. Because of the high temperatures during the summer, most of the work on the bridge was done at night using flood-lights. Since it was nearly impossible to load the cables on pack animals, other arrangements had to be made. The problem was solved when, one at a time, the eight steel supporting cables and the two wind cables were carried from the rim to the river on the shoulders of 42 Havasupai Indians stationed at intervals along the trail.

As you cross the bridge, look upstream and you will see the U.S.G.S. Gauging Station. Look downstream and you will see a sandy area formed at the confluence of Bright Angel Creek and the Colorado River.

South Kaibab Trail

Bright Angel Campground, the Phantom Ranch, and the North Kaibab Trail—Once you cross the Colorado River, the trail passes by ruins of an old Pueblo Indian settlement, turns down river toward Bright Angel Creek and then follows Bright Angel Creek upstream. To reach Bright Angel Campground, cross a small bridge spanning the creek. The River Ranger Station and the campground are located here on the west bank of the creek. If you want to go to Phantom Ranch, do not cross the creek. Instead, follow the trail upstream about 0.5 mile (0.8 kilometer). South Kaibab Trail and North Kaibab Trail join at the Phantom Ranch area. More information about Phantom Ranch and the North Kaibab Trail can be found on pages 56 and 95, respectively.

South Kaibab Trail

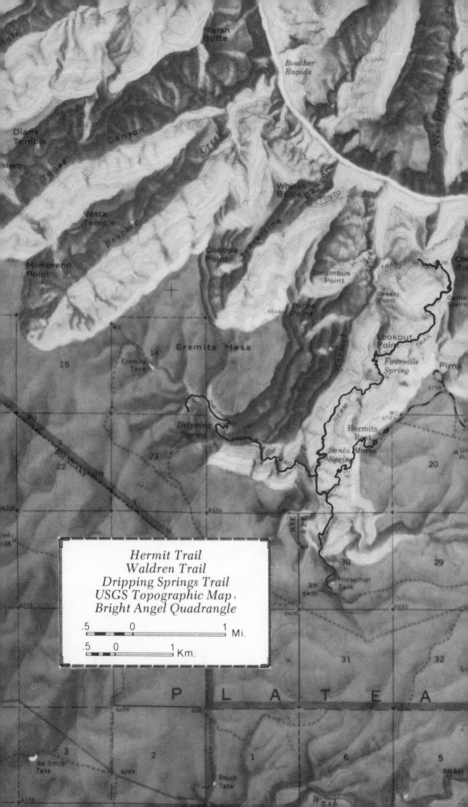

Hermit Trail
Waldren Trail
Dripping Springs Trail
USGS Topographic Map ,
Bright Angel Quadrangle

Wilderness Trails—Good Condition

Hermit Trail, Waldren Trail, Dripping Springs Trail

Since Ralph Cameron controlled Bright Angel Trail and charged a fee for using it, Fred Harvey decided to build another trail to the Colorado River for his tourist trade. The result was Hermit Trail. From 1912 to 1930, the Sante Fe Railroad provided overnight accommodations for tourists at Hermit Camp located near Hermit Creek and about an hour's walk from the Colorado River. The camp consisted mostly of tents but had the convenience of piped water. Supplies could be brought down from Pima Point via an aerial tram. Hermit Camp was abandoned when the Phantom Ranch was constructed in 1922. Hermit Trail was maintained by the Park Service until 1931.

The Hermit trailhead can be found by taking the West Rim Drive to Hermit's Rest then following the fire lane just west of the parking lot.

Although Hermit Trail is still in relatively good condition, expect to encounter rock slides, especially in the Supai Group. From the trailhead to Hermit Camp, the distance is approximately 7 miles (11.3 kilometers). It is another 1.5 miles (2.4 kilometers) from Hermit Camp to the Colorado River. Two short side trails, Waldren Trail and Dripping Springs Trail, connect with Hermit Trail.

> *Waldren Trail Junction*—Hermit Trail descends to Hermit Basin, a distance of approximately 1 mile (1.6 kilometers), where you will see a side trail going to the south. This is Waldren Trail which travels about 1.5 miles (2.4 kilometers) through the Basin and then up to the South Rim. At the rim, follow the trail for another 0.5 mile (.8 kilometer) and you will find Horsethief Tank and a fire road.

> *Dripping Springs Trail Junction*—A short distance below the junction of Hermit and Waldren Trails, you will find a side trail going to the northwest. This trail follows a cliff for about 1.5 miles (2.4 kilometers) to Dripping Springs, a normally reliable water source.

> *Santa Maria Spring and Resthouse*—If you continue north on Hermit Trail at the junction of Dripping Springs Trail, you will find Santa Maria Spring. The spring, located just above the resthouse at the foot of the Coconino Formation, is normally a reliable source of water. However, as a precaution it is advisable to purify the water before drinking. At this point the trail begins to descend gradually

through the Supai Group. Rock slides have taken their toll along this portion of the trail and Four Mile Spring can't be found.

Tonto Trail Junction—You will descend the Redwall on a series of switchbacks known as Cathedral Stairs. As you do, look for Cope Butte ahead and to the right. The trail passes by Cope Butte and at its base you will find the junction of Tonto Trail. Turning right (northeast) on Tonto Trail will take you to Indian Gardens. Follow Hermit Trail (westerly) and you will find the remains of the old Hermit Camp.

Hermit Creek Campsite—Just beyond the old Hermit Camp, a campsite with a chemical toilet has been established. Water is normally available in Hermit Creek but be sure to purify it. The ecosystem is rather fragile in this area so please take care not to disrupt it.

Hermit Rapids—From the campsite you can follow Hermit Creek to the Colorado River. Here you will be treated to the sights and sounds of Hermit Rapids, one of the most dangerous rapids in the river.

Tonto Trail

If you are a very experienced wilderness backpacker and would like to explore more of the length of the Grand Canyon rather than just the routes leading from the rim to the Colorado River, Tonto Trail provides this opportunity. Tonto Trail is not a rim-to-river route but traverses the Tonto Platform for 72 miles (116 kilometers) from Garnet Canyon on the west to Red Canyon on the east. In so doing, it connects many of the rim-to-river trails.

Although some sections of the trail are in better condition than others, topography, wild burro trails, and general erosion make this trail generally difficult to follow. Water and lack of shade are also major concerns on the Tonto as springs are often unreliable and difficult to locate. However, water can normally be found in Boucher, Hance, Hermit and Monument Creeks.

Two sections of Tonto Trail are in better condition and easier to follow than the rest: between Hermit Trail and Plateau Point/Indian Gardens, a distance of about 12.3 miles (19.8 kilometers); and between South Kaibab Trail and Bright Angel Trail (Indian Gardens area), a distance of about 4.6 miles (7.4 kilometers).

Tonto Trail
Western Section
Garnet Canyon to
Slate Creek Area
USGS Topographic Map
Havasupai Point Quadrangle

.5   0   1 Mi.

.5   0   1 Km.

Hotauta
Canyon

Evans
Butte

Amphitheater

COLORADO

Monadnock
Amphitheater

RIVER

Le Conte
Plateau

Scorpion Ridge

Slate

Creek

Tuna

Bass
Plateau

GRANITE

GORGE

Canyon

Crystal
Rapids

Canyon

Agate

Geikie
Peak

Scylla
Butte

Creek

Castor
Temple

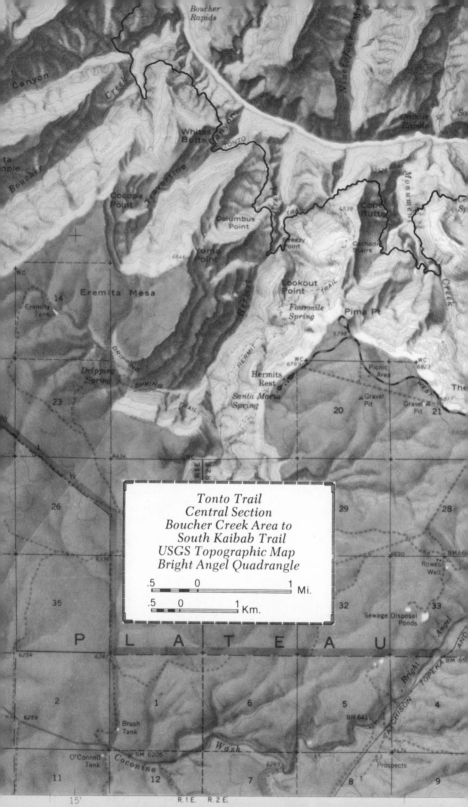

Tonto Trail
Central Section
Boucher Creek Area to
South Kaibab Trail
USGS Topographic Map
Bright Angel Quadrangle

.5   0   1 Mi.

.5   0   1 Km.

Tonto Trail
Eastern Section
South Kaibab Trail to
Hance Trail (Red Canyon)
USGS Topographic Maps
Bright Angel Quadrangle
Vishnu Temple Quadrangle

.5   0   1 Mi.

.5   0   1 Km.

Angels Window

Cape Royal

Freya Castle

Angels Gate

Vishnu Temple

Dunn Butte

5714

Krishna Shrine

Rama Shrine

6411

Hall Butte

Hawkins Butte

Vishnu

Newberry Butte

Asbestos Canyon

Spring

Sheba Temple

5070

Sockdolager Rapids

COLORADO

Hance Rapids

BM 2608

Spring

Cottonwood

TONTO

TRAIL

TONTO

Canyon

2993

Cave

Hance

Ayer Point

Mineral

Red

Horseshoe Mesa

Creek

Spring

4400

BM 3689

O'Neill Spr

Spring

GRANDVIEW

Hance

BM

BM 4949

Moran Point

Coronado

Wilderness Trails—Fair Condition

Tanner Trail

Like many trails in the Canyon, the Tanner Trail was an improvement on existing Indian routes. Until about 1912, the Hopi Indians were quite active in the eastern part of the Canyon. They often visited a ceremonial salt deposit near the Colorado River below the mouth of the Little Colorado River. The Hopi's Sipapu (entrance to the underworld) is located in the canyon of the Little Colorado River about 4.5 miles (7 kilometers) above the confluence of the two rivers.

John D. Lee's lost gold mine is also rumored to be in this area of the Canyon. John D. Lee established Lee's Ferry about 1871 but was convicted in 1874 and executed in 1877 for his part in a massacre of a group of pioneers in Mountain Meadows. If there was gold, Lee took his secret to his grave because no one has ever found the hidden gold.

In 1880, Seth B. Tanner, a Mormon settler from Tuba City, organized the Little Colorado Mining District. By following the old Hopi trails, he found a little copper along the Colorado River. He improved the trail adding the upper section during the 1890s. Remnants of the mining activities can still be seen.

Tanner Trail was also used by a gang of thieves who would steal horses in Arizona, bring them down Tanner Trail, change their brands, move them across the Colorado River and up Nankoweap Trail to sell them in Utah. After making the sale, the thieves would steal more horses, this time in Utah and herd them down the Nankoweap, across the river, up the Tanner and into Arizona where they knew they had a market. This activity went on for years and the Tanner-Nankoweap Trail rim-to-rim connection became known as Horsethief Trail.

To find the trailhead, take East Rim Drive to Lipan Point. The trailhead is about 100 yards (91 meters) east of the point.

The trail to the river is difficult to follow at times but some rock cairns have been placed at important points along the way. Keep in mind, however, that you cannot always rely on cairns to remain in place. The distance to the Colorado River is 8 miles (12.9 kilometers) and there is no water available until you reach the river.

The trail descends quickly to the slopes of Escalante and Cardenas Buttes. After following the slopes for about 3 miles (4.8 kilometers), the trail descends the Redwall via a set of switchbacks. The trail then descends slowly to Tanner Wash and becomes rather narrow as the lower part of the trail passes through the red shale.

Plateu Point Trail

Tanner Trail
USGS Topographic Map
Vishnu Temple Quadrangle

Grandview Trail

Copper was found at the base of Horseshoe Mesa in 1890. Pete Berry quickly established his "Last Chance Copper Mine" and by 1892 he was building a trail from Grandview Point to the mining area.

In 1895, the Grandview Hotel, a two-story log building was constructed near the head of Berry's trail and became a busy tourist center. When the Santa Fe brought the railroad to the present Grand Canyon Village in 1901 and built the El Tovar Hotel, business at the Grandview rapidly declined. The final death blow to the area came when the mines no longer showed a profit. With the mines and the hotel closed, the trail was used only infrequently and finally abandoned.

To find the trailhead, take the East Rim Drive to Grandview Point. The trailhead is just north of the parking lot.

The distance to Horseshoe Mesa is about 3 miles (4.8 kilometers) over a trail that is in fairly good condition and not too difficult. Part of the trail still shows evidence of an earlier paving technique consisting of fitting rocks together edgewise. This type of construction was rather time-consuming but resulted in a very durable trail surface.

There are three trails leading off Horseshoe Mesa to the Tonto Trail. All three are steep and very difficult. There is no water on the Mesa, but a spring can be found on a short side trail near the base of the east side trail. Camping is not allowed in this area so continue downstream for about 2 miles (3.2 kilometers) to the Tonto Trail and Hance Canyon where water is also available and camping is permitted.

On the west side of the Mesa you can follow the trail into Cottonwood Canyon. Water can be found in the west fork of the south arm. You will also find the remains of an old camp. Getting to the Colorado River from west of Horseshoe Mesa is rather difficult. A side trail leading west of Cottonwood Creek does exist but it is extremely difficult to locate. Other routes from the mouth of Cottonwood Creek are possible, but also difficult to locate. It is most advisable to check with the Backcountry Office to receive an update on the condition of these routes to the River.

South Bass Trail

In 1883, William Wallace Bass moved from New York to Williams, Arizona for his health. The rumor about Lee's lost gold mine prompted him to visit the Canyon. The Canyon made such an impression on Bass that he decided to set up camp near Havasupai Point. In 1890, he built a road to Ashfork. While living at the Grand Canyon, Bass played the violin, wrote poetry, took photographs, prospected, lectured, guided tours, built trails, operated a stage line and installed cable ways across the Colorado River. Bass was also instrumental in helping the Havasupai Indians establish their first school. The trail was used by Bass in the 1890s as an access to his asbestos and copper mines. When Bass died in 1933, his ashes were scattered over Holy Grail Temple, often called Bass Tomb.

The trailhead is located in the western part of the park about 4 miles (6.4 kilometers) north of Pasture Wash Ranger Station. Since the dirt roads leading to Bass Camp and the trailhead are subject to heavy mud in the spring, snow in the winter and general erosion at other times, check at Park Headquarters for up-to-date information on the conditions of the roads and driving instuctions. Even under normal conditions, you will need a four-wheel drive vehicle or a truck with lots of ground clearance.

The only reliable source of water is the Colorado River. The distance from rim to river is about 9 miles (14.5 kilometers). The trail is in fair condition and is generally easy to follow through the Kaibab and Coconino Formations. As the trail turns northwesterly across the plateau in Hermit Shale, it becomes difficult to follow and the switchbacks in the Supai Formation are nearly gone. But as the trail turns southerly it improves somewhat and becomes easier to follow. In Bass Canyon, the trail is covered in places by brush. The trail, after some criss-crossing, takes you to the east side of Bass Canyon along the slope. When you reach the dryfall above the Colorado River, the trail goes westerly out of the creek bed and then down to the river.

Various Strata on South Rim

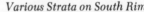

Grandview Trail
USGS Topographic Maps
Vishnu Temple Quadrangle
Grandview Point Quadrangle

.5   0   1 Mi.

.5   0   1 Km.

South Bass Trail
USGS Topographic Map
Havasupai Point Quadrangle

.5   0   1 Mi.
.5   0   1 Km.

Wilderness Trails—Bad Condition

New Hance Trail (Red Canyon Trail)

"Captain" John Hance came to the Grand Canyon around 1883 and built a log cabin east of Grandview Point. Although he worked an asbestos mine across the Colorado River, he was best known as a trailbuilder, tourist guide and storyteller. In 1906, Hance sold the last of his Grand Canyon property and moved into the Bright Angel Hotel as resident Grand Canyon character. He received room and board for just entertaining the tourists by telling yarns about his experiences in the Grand Canyon.

Much of Hance's original trail, Old Hance Trail, located near his cabin was virtually destroyed by rock slides in 1894. Rather than trying to rebuild the trail, he built a new one farther east into Red Canyon.

To find the trailhead, take the East Rim Drive to 1 mile (1.6 kilometers) southwest of the Moran Point turnoff. You will find a rather indistinct car track leading away from the drive. Follow the track until you come to a shallow drainage area to the left. Stay in the draw and you will soon find a cairn marking the trailhead. The distance to the Colorado River is about 8 miles (12.9 kilometers), with the river being the only reliable source of water.

This is a very difficult, steep and rocky trail. Although some cairns mark the way, you will find yourself spending a lot of time searching for the trail, especially in the Supai Formation and along the rim of the Redwall. The descent in the Redwall is extremely difficult to find and some hikers have followed deer trails down when they have been unable to locate the break. The trail improves somewhat through the Tonto slope but you will encounter a confusing network of wild burro trails. Below Moran Point, the trail passes a major side canyon entering from the southeast then descends into the bed of Red Canyon. The trail then follows the bed to the Colorado River and Hance Rapids.

Boucher Trail

Louis D. Boucher came to the Grand Canyon from Canada around 1891. He established a home camp at Dripping Springs and another camp in Long (Boucher) Canyon where he grew tomatoes, other vegetables, and fruits. He also had a copper mine and tourist cabins near his orchard.

Boucher was called "The Hermit" probably because he was known to be rather quiet and spent most of his time either at his base camp at Dripping Springs or at his orchard. Boucher's original trail was called the Silver Bell Trail.

To reach what is left of Boucher Trail, follow Hermit Trail to

Dripping Springs Trail then follow Dripping Springs Trail for about 1 mile (1.6 kilometers) until you cross a major drainage area coming from the west. Boucher Trail goes north along a shelf on top of the Supai Formation.

As you approach the head of Travertine Canyon, about 1 mile (1.6 kilometers) beyond Columbus Point, look for small rock cairns. At this point the trail becomes difficult to follow as it descends through the Hermit and Supai Formations to the top of the Redwall. The trail crosses Whites Butte Saddle then descends the Redwall steeply. The trail then becomes somewhat easier to follow at the base of Whites Butte and soon meets the Tonto Trail. Follow the trail to a point just before you reach Boucher Creek and you will find the ruins of Boucher's camp south of the trail. To reach the Colorado River, follow Boucher Creek.

The distance from Hermit's Rest to Boucher Creek is approximately 11 miles (17.7 kilometers). Water can normally be found at Dripping Springs, Boucher Creek and, of course, the Colorado River.

The South Rim Trail

Although there is no substitute for actually hiking into the depths of the Grand Canyon, viewing the Canyon from the South Rim and exploring some of the areas along the rim itself can also be most rewarding experiences. The South Rim Trail provides this opportunity. It generally follows along the edge of the South Rim for about 9 miles (14 kilometers) from Mather Point on the east through the Grand Canyon Village area to Hermit's Rest on the west. From Maricopa Point to Yavapai Point the trail is paved. Also, the Canyon Shuttle Bus serves the major points from Yavapai Point to Hermit's Rest making the return trip by foot unnecessary in many cases. Self-guiding pamphlets for some sections of the Rim Trail are available at the Visitors Center. Although some of the best views of the Canyon can be found along the route between Hermit's Rest and Mather Point, a continuation of the trail moves southeasterly then northeasterly for about 2.5 miles (4.1 kilometers) from Mather Point to the South Kaibab Trailhead and then northward from the trailhead for about .5 mile (.8 kilometer) to Yaki Point. Yaki Point also provides excellent views.

New Hance Trail
(Red Canyon Trail)
USGS Topographic Maps
Vishnu Temple Quadrangle
Grandview Point Quadrangle

.5   0   1 Mi.

.5   0   1 Km.

Boucher Trail (via Hermit Trail and Dripping Springs Trail)
USGS Topographic Map
Bright Angel Quadrangle

.5   0   1 Mi.

.5   0   1 Km.

South Rim Trail
USGS Topographic Map
Bright Angel Quadrangle

.5   0   1 Mi.

.5   0   1 Km.

Code For NASA Landstat Photo of Grand Canyon

1. Grand Canyon Village (South Rim Developed Area)
2. North Rim Developed Area
3. Desert View Area
4. Havasu Canyon (Havasupai Area)

North Rim

Chapter 7

The North Rim

General Information

Due to the heavy snowfalls, the North Rim is only open from about mid-May through about mid-October. The area is much less developed than the South Rim and provides fewer facilities and more solitude for visitors. Many of the trailheads are located outside of the developed area of the North Rim requiring some traveling over rather primitive roads. The only entrance to the developed area of the North Rim of the Grand Canyon National Park is located on Arizona 67 approximately 32 miles (51 kilometers) south of U.S. 89A at Jacob Lake, Arizona.

Food And Lodging Outside The Park

Kaibab Lodge

Located 5 miles (8 kilometers) north of the North Rim Entrance on Arizona Highway 67, the Kaibab Lodge is the nearest out-of-park motel and dining facility. Telephone: (602) 638-2389.

Jacob Lake Area

Food and lodging are also available at Jacob Lake located 13 miles

(21 kilometers) north of the North Rim Entrance Station at the junction of U.S. 89A and Arizona 67.

Food And Lodging Inside The Park

Grand Canyon Lodge

The Grand Canyon Lodge is located about 13 miles (21 kilometers) south of the Entrance Station. It provides a full range of accommodations including a dining room, buffeteria and coffee shop, patio lounge, and a western saloon. For reservations contact:

> T.W.A. Services
> 451 North Main
> Cedar City, Utah
> Telephone: (801) 586-7686

Camping Inside The Park

North Rim Campground

Operated on a first come, first served basis, this campground provides showers, a laundry, and a general store.

Camping Outside The Park

DeMotte Campground

The campground located about 5 miles (8 kilometers) north of the North Rim Entrance Station, has only 20 sites. It is operated by the U.S. Forest Service on a first come, first served basis.

Jacob Lake Campground

Also operated by the U.S. Forest Service on a first come, first served basis, this campground is located about 30 miles (48 kilometers) north of the North Rim Entrance Station at the junction of U.S. 89A and Arizona 67. Water, restrooms and trailer dumping facilities are available.

Other campgrounds are located near trailheads. They will be discussed under the section presenting the trails.

Inner Canyon Trails And Camping

Reservations and General Information

The same regulations apply to trails and camping on routes

emanating from the North Rim as those applying to South Rim trips. For example, overnight hiking reservations and permits are required; no fires below the rim; gain experience on maintained trails before hiking the wilderness trails. Roads leading from the only paved road to some trailheads may not be passible due to weather conditions. The address and telephone number of the Backcountry Reservation Office is found on page 49. You can pick up your permit and obtain additional up-to-date information about the condition of North Rim roads and trails at the National Park Service Information Desk located in the Grand Canyon Lodge, North Rim or at the Information Station located at Jacob Lake.

Maintained Trail

North Kaibab Trail

To complete the new rim-to-rim route, the top portion of North Kaibab Trail was finished in 1927. The portion below Manzanita Point generally follows the Old Bright Angel Trail (Old Kaibab Trail) route, while the portion above Manzanita Point traveled a new route through Roaring Springs Canyon. Additional historical information about the construction of the Kaibab Trail can be found on page 97.

The trailhead is located just south of the paved road at a point about 2 miles (3.2 kilometers) north of the Grand Canyon Lodge and about 11 miles (17.7 kilometers) south of the Entrance Station.

North Kaibab Trail is the only maintained North Rim inner canyon route. It is usually in excellent condition and well-marked. However, heavy winter snows, flash floods, and rock slides occasionally block or destroy parts of the trail. It is advisable to inquire at the Park Service Information Desk about the condition of the trail before you begin your hike. The distance from the trailhead to the Colorado River is 14 miles (22.5 kilometers). Information about important landmarks follow:

> *Roaring Springs Campground*—From the rim the trail descends Roaring Springs Canyon to Roaring Springs. The trail is rather steep and presents several challenging switchbacks. As you near the campground, you will be able to hear the water coming from Roaring Springs. The water flows from a cave containing nearly 11,000 feet (3,353 meters) of passages. You will also see several buildings and the pumphouse that supplies water to the North Rim and to the South Rim through a trans-canyon pipeline. The campground, which is only open April through October, provides water, tables and toilets. The distance from the trailhead is about 4.7 miles (7.6 kilometers).

Old Bright Angel Trail (Old Kaibab Trail) Junction—Emergency Telephone—A short distance below the Roaring Springs Campground area the trail crosses Bright Angel Creek. Just before you reach the bridge you will find some buildings and an emergency telephone near the creek. After you cross the bridge, you will see Old Bright Angel Trail (Old Kaibab Trail) on your left (northeastly).

Cottonwood Campground—The distance from Roaring Springs to Cottonwood Campground is a relatively easy 2.1 miles (3.4 kilometers). The campground is near the creek and offers water, tables and toilets. It is only open April through October.

Ribbon Falls—A short side trail leading across Bright Angel Creek by bridge to Ribbon Falls can be found at about 1.8 miles (2.9 kilometers) below Cottonwood. This area is quite beautiful but fragile, especially the travertine formation at the base of the falls. Take time to enjoy but please leave it undisturbed. To return to the Kaibab Trail you can follow the side trail downstream a short distance and then cross Bright Angel Creek. If the water in the Bright Angel is high, you may want to return upstream to the bridge.

Phantom Ranch And Bright Angel Campground—The distance from Cottonwood to the Phantom Ranch is 5.5 miles (8.9 kilometers). It is another 1.8 miles (2.9 kilometers) to the Colorado River from Phantom Ranch. Bright Angel Campground is below Phantom Ranch near the confluence of Bright Angel Creek and the Colorado River.

From Cottonwood to the Colorado River, the trail generally parallels Bright Angel Creek and crosses it four times. The descent is more or less gradual and walking near the creek provides an opportunity to cool off whenever necessary.

At Phantom Ranch a snack bar is usually open and water is available. To locate Bright Angel Campground, follow the trail through the Phantom Ranch cottage area and past the corrals. Continue downstream for a short distance and you will see a bridge crossing Bright Angel Creek. As you cross the bridge, the campground is to your right along the creek. The Ranger Station and other buildings are nearby to your left. Water, tables, and toilets are available on a year-round basis. For historical information about the area, see page 56.

Wilderness Trails—Fair Condition

Clear Creek Trail

In the mid-1930s, during the time the River Trail and the rim-to-rim Kaibab Trails were being constructed by the Civilian Conservation Corps, the National Park Service had the Corps also build a trail from the Phantom Ranch area to Clear Creek. Not established to be used by mules, Clear Creek provided fishing and a view of Cheyava Falls for adventurous hikers. Although Cheyava Falls remains, the fishing is far less reliable.

The trailhead begins about 0.3 mile (.48 kilometer) north of Phantom Ranch on the North Kaibab Trail. Clear Creek Trail, although not maintained, is in fair condition and easy to follow. There is no dependable water source until you reach Clear Creek. This is a long, hot (no shade), and rather monotonous trip with most of the reward coming at the end when you finally reach the waters of Clear Creek, some 8.7 miles (14.0 kilometers) from the trailhead.

The trail moves easily from Bright Angel Creek up to the Tonto Plateau. Once on the Plateau, the trail moves generally in a southeasterly direction, occasionally cutting around a side canyon or drainage area, until it reaches an area below Demaray Point. Here the trail swings northerly around and below the Point and then easterly across Zoroaster Canyon, eventually turning northerly and then again easterly as it drops down into Clear Creek.

Once at Clear Creek, you can explore the area in either direction. It is possible to reach the Colorado River by following Clear Creek, but there is no trail. The route to the River can be rather dangerous because of the polished granite, some straight cliff walls and sudden drops.

Regardless of where you explore or camp in the Clear Creek area, stay alert to the possibility of flash floods. Flash floods can happen even if it is not raining in your location. It is best to camp high and away from the Creek bed.

Old Bright Angel Trail (Old Kaibab Trail)

In the early 1900s tourism suffered on the North Rim because of poor access roads and heavy winter snows. In order to bring tourists from the "booming" South Rim to the North Rim, "Uncle Dee" Wooley from Kanab, Utah, and his son-in-law, David Rust, had the "Old Kaibab" Trail built. The trail through Bright Angel Canyon to the Colorado River was an improvement on the route used earlier by Francois Matthes, a geologist. By 1907, the trail crossed the Colorado River near the mouth of the Bright Angel Creek via a cable and cage apparatus. It then went up to the Tonto Platform at the Tipoff and

North Kaibab Trail
Old Bright Angel Trail (Old
Kaibab Trail)
Clear Creek Trail
USGS Topographic Map.
Bright Angel Quadrangle

.5   0   1 Mi.

.5   0   1 Km.

over to Indian Gardens where it connected with the Cameron-controlled Bright Angel Trail. This route was used until the 1930s when the River and new rim-to-rim Kaibab Trails were completed.

The portion of the Old Kaibab Trail below Manzanita Point was improved and became part of the new North Kaibab Trail. The upper portion of the Old Kaibab Trail was essentially abandoned when the new trail into Roaring Springs Canyon was completed in 1927.

To reach the trailhead, follow the paved road northeast past the "Y" intersection to the Fuller Canyon E-2 Fire Road. Since private vehicles are prohibited on this fire road, you will have to walk about 2.0 miles (3.2 kilometers) along E-2 until it ends at the trailhead. You can also reach the trailhead by following a forest trail leading northeast from the North Kaibab Trailhead. The distance from one trailhead to the other via this wooded trail is about 3.5 miles (5.6 kilometers).

The Old Bright Angel Trail is in fair condition and usually not too difficult to follow. Water is available at Bright Angel Creek and Roaring Springs. The distance from the trailhead to Roaring Springs is about 7.0 miles (11.3 kilometers).

Parts of the trail along the upper portion are hidden by brush and scrub-oak, but you can usually locate the trail in spite of the vegetation. The trail switchbacks through the Coconino Formation, fairly well straightens out for awhile, then switchbacks down the Redwall. Surprisingly, the switchbacks remain in fairly good condition. Once the trail drops to the Bright Angel Creek, it follows the west bank then crosses the creek at about 0.5 mile (0.8 kilometer) above the juncture of the Bright Angel and Roaring Springs Creeks.

The Old Bright Angel Trail connects with the North Kaibab Trail on the west side of the Bright Angel Creek about 0.1 mile (1.6 kilometers) below the juncture of Roaring Springs and Bright Angel Creeks. An emergency telephone is located near the Kaibab Trail just north of the bridge on the west side of the creek. Follow the Kaibab Trail to the north about 1.5 miles (2.4 kilometers) and you will reach Roaring Springs Campground. Follow the Kaibab Trail to the south for about 2.0 miles (3.2 kilometers) and you will reach Cottonwood Campground.

Wilderness Trails—Fair To Poor Condition

Thunder River Trail

Although Thunder River probably holds the dubious distinction of being the shortest river in the world, it does not come up short in the loudest noise category. You see, Thunder River begins as dual spouts of water shooting from a cliff about 100 feet (30.5 meters) high then it crashes, roars, thunders and cascades its way over an incredibly short

0.5 mile (0.8 kilometer) course until it empties into Tapeats Creek. It is, indeed, a spectacular display in such a short distance.

There are two converging routes from the North Rim to Thunder River. The shortest route is Thunder River Trail which begins near Monument Point while the other trail begins near the campground in Indian Hollow. The trails converge below and southwest of Monument Point. Both trails are in fair condition and generally easy to follow. The original Thunder River Trail was completed in 1926 by the Civilian Conservation Corps. No water is available on either trail until you reach Thunder River.

If you choose to take the longer route, you will find the trailhead a short distance southwest of Indian Hollow Campground in the Kaibab National Forest. From the rim, the trail goes westerly past Little Saddle, then swings back in an easterly direction until it crosses Deer Creek. At this point the trail moves southwesterly until it joins with Thunder River Trail coming from Monument Point.

To reach the Thunder River trailhead at Monument Point go to the west end of Forest Service Road #292A in the Big Saddle area of the Kaibab National Forest. The distance from the trailhead to the junction of Thunder River and Tapeats Creek is about 7.5 miles (12.1 kilometers). It is another 2.5 miles (4.0 kilometers) from this junction to the Colorado River.

From the rim, the trail moves from the east to the west side of Monument Point before dropping quickly through the Kaibab and Toroweap Formations then it continues westerly below Monument Point to the top of the Supai. Swinging southwesterly, the trail winds around several drainage areas then descends the Redwall via several short switchbacks. The trail continues south to a bowl-shaped area called Surprise Valley. As the trail turns easterly, you will find a side trail leading westerly to Deer Creek. (After the side trail reaches Deer Creek, it follows the creekbed on the westside then turns west and descends to the Colorado River at Deer Creek Falls.)

To reach Thunder River, avoid the side trail and continue east. When you reach the northeast rim of Surprise Valley you should be able to see and hear Thunder River. The trail follows Thunder River on the south until it reaches a camping area at Tapeats Creek. Since this area is subject to flash floods, camp high and away from the water.

The trail from the Thunder River and Tapeats Creek junction to the Colorado River is marked by cairns. This is a rather rough and potentially dangerous trail as you will have to cross Tapeats Creek twice: west side to east side about 0.5 mile (.80 kilometer) below the junction and back to the west side after about another 1.0 mile (1.6 kilometers). Switchbacks on the west side of the creek will bring you to the Colorado River near Tapeats Rapids.

Thunder River Trail
Deer Creek Trail
USGS Topographic Maps
Powell Plateau Quadrangle
Kanab Point Quadrangle

.5   0   1 Mi.

.5   0   1 Km.

Lava Falls Trail

About one million years ago volcanic activity in the western part of the Grand Canyon blocked the Colorado River with a dam of lava about 500 feet (152 meters) high, creating a huge lake. The lake is gone now but incredible remnants of the lava flow and dam still remain at Vulcan's Throne and Lava Falls (Vulcan Rapid).

Lava Falls is located in the former Grand Canyon National Monument. Depending upon from which direction you are arriving, you will need to travel between about 50 to 70 miles (81 to 113 kilometers) on graded or unimproved roads to reach Toroweap Viewpoint Road and Vulcan's Throne. The best route is to take the Mt. Trumbell Recreation Area Road just a few miles southwest of Fredonia, Arizona on Arizona 389. A longer, more difficult and confusing route can be found at St. George, Utah connecting with U.S. 15. Since these routes are subject to change due to weather conditions and other factors, be sure to inquire about specific instructions and the condition of the roads before you begin your trip.

To reach the trailhead, go west from Toroweap Viewpoint Road to the western base of Vulcan's Throne. Although there is no constructed trail, the trailhead and the route are well marked with cairns. The route is very steep and rocky as it moves across the ancient lava flow so be prepared for a rather rugged trip. There is no water until you reach the Colorado River. The distance from the trailhead to the river is about 1.5 miles (2.4 kilometers). Two campgrounds are located above the river east of Vulcan's Throne toward Saddle Horse Canyon.

Tuckup Trail

If the South Rim Tonto Trail has a North Rim counterpart, it is the Tuckup Trail. Neither trail is a rim-to-river route and each traverses part of the length of the Canyon above the Colorado River. Tuckup Trail, located within the former Grand Canyon National Monument, generally follows along the Esplande between lower Toroweap Valley on the west and Boysag Point on the east. Although the trail is somewhat difficult to find in places, most of its 64 miles (103 kilometers) can still be followed.

Tuckup Trail has three fairly reliable water sources and three seasonal sources. The reliable sources are June Spring at Willow Canyon, Cottonwood Spring at Cottonwood Canyon, and Schmutz Spring southwest of Tuckup Canyon. The seasonal sources, Tule, Dome and Cork Springs, are dependable only in the spring and only if there was sufficient precipitation during the winter. Some water pockets can also be found along the trail.

Tuckup Trail provides access to several interesting points along its route such as Saddle Horse, Cone, Stairway, Fern Glen and Tuckup

Canyons. However, exploring these areas should only be attempted by skilled backcountry hikers. In some cases equipment for climbing is required. Routes into these areas are often obscure, very difficult and dangerous. Check with the Backcountry Office for details before planning any trip into these side canyons.

Tuckup Trail also provides access to a dome-like formation located between Fern Glen and Tuckup Canyons. Dome Trail goes south from the Tuckup Trail and then completely encircles the Dome.

View from behind Ribbon Falls on the North Kaibab Trail

Lava Falls Trail
USGS Topographic Map
Vulcans Throne Quadrangle

.5   0   1
                                           Mi.

.5   0   1 Km.

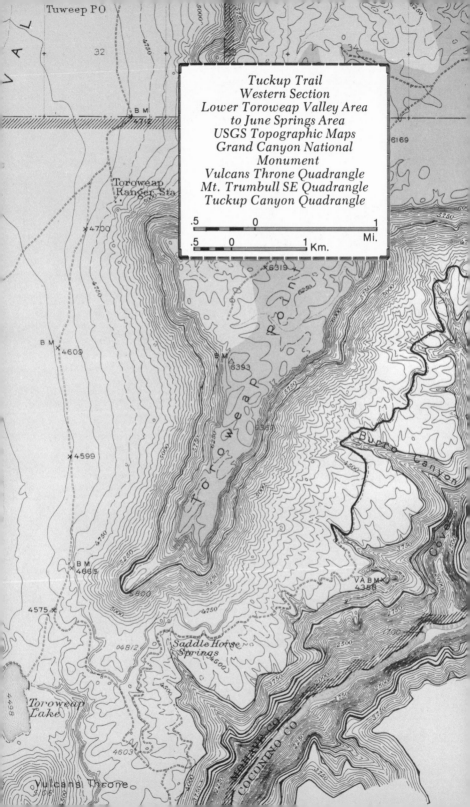

Tuckup Trail
Western Section
Lower Toroweap Valley Area
to June Springs Area
USGS Topographic Maps
Grand Canyon National
Monument
Vulcans Throne Quadrangle
Mt. Trumbull SE Quadrangle
Tuckup Canyon Quadrangle

.5   0   1
.5   0   1 Km.   Mi.

Tuweep PO

Toroweap
Ranger Sta.

Saddle Horse
Springs

Toroweap
Lake

Vulcans Throne

COCONINO CO

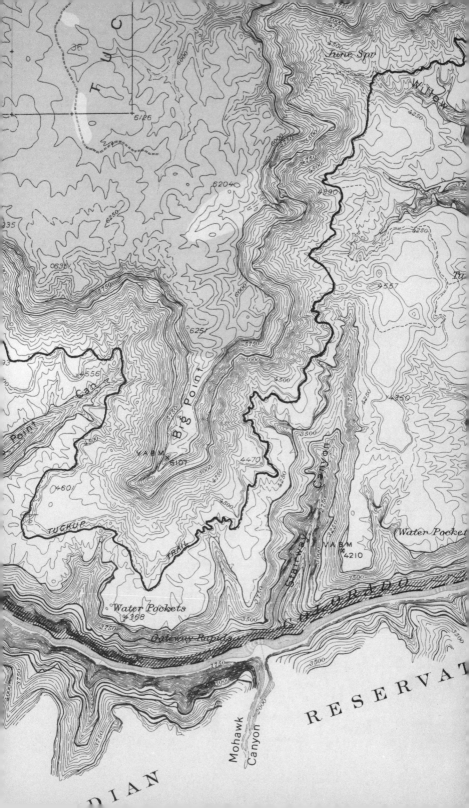

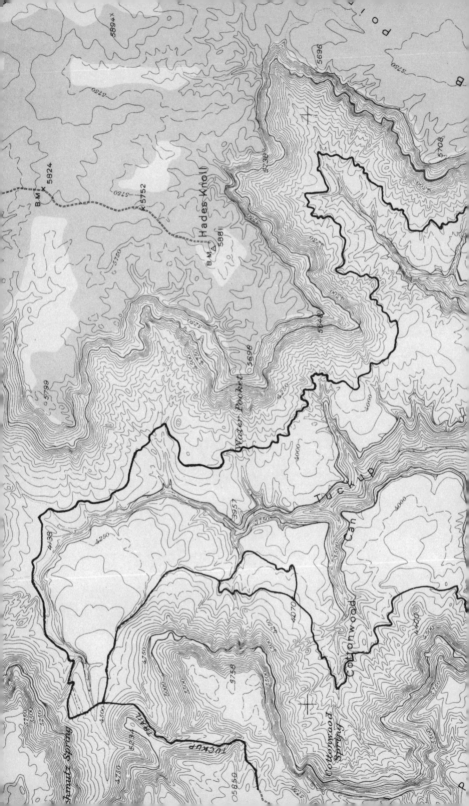

Tuckup Trail
Central Section and Dome Trail
USGS Topographic Maps
Grand Canyon National
Monument
Tuckup Canyon Quadrangle

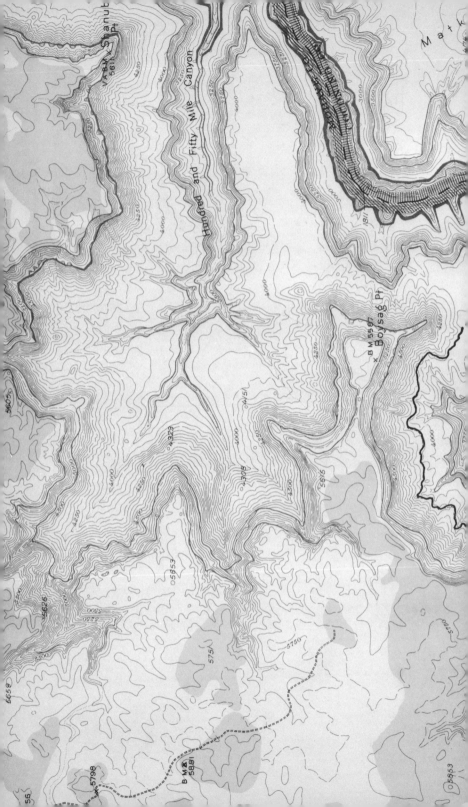

Tuckup Trail
Eastern Section
The Cork Area to Boysag
Point Area
USGS Topographic Maps
Grand Canyon National
Monument
Tuckup Canyon Quadrangle
Kanab Point Quadrangle

.5   0   1 Mi.

.5   0   1 Km.

SINYALA MESA

Sinyala Canyon

Sinyala Rapids

Tuckup Canyon

Tuckup Canyon

Yumtheska Mesa

Wet Weather Seep

3983

3967

3975

4000

4055

Boysag Rapids

VABM
3952

VABM
3957

The Cork
4347

TRAIL

Cork Spring

Water Pocket

Water Pocket

4087

4000

3250

3750

4010

Wilderness Trails—Bad Condition

North Bass Trail

W.W. Bass was active on both sides of the Colorado River and established a camp on the North Rim side of the river where he grew vegetables and other crops. Historical information about Bass can be found on page 76.

The Denver, Colorado Canyon and Pacific Railroad Company was formed in 1889 for the purpose of building a railroad from Denver *through* the Grand Canyon to San Diego. An open area north of Bass Rapid was selected by R.B. Stanton, the chief engineer for the project, as the site for the railroad's switchyard. Stanton was chosen to determine the best route for the railroad because of his remarkable success with the Georgetown Loop in Colorado. Most of his survey trips down the Colorado River ended in disasters but he persisted and eventually gathered enough information to convince him that a trans-canyon railroad could be built. However, others were more skeptical and the project never proceeded beyond the initial planning stages.

The trailhead is located at Swamp Point near the west end of the fire road serving the Swamp Ridge area. Water is usually available at Muav Saddle Spring and, of course, the Colorado River. The distance from the trailhead to the Colorado River is about 14 miles (22.5 kilometers).

The trail from Swamp Point down to Muav Saddle is not too difficult to follow. At Muav Saddle you will find a side trail going southwesterly. (This trail leads to the west of Muav Saddle and then southerly onto the Powell Plateau.) The Bass Trail continues easterly just a short distance to the bottom of the Coconino where you will find Muav Saddle Spring. Beyond the spring, the trail follows the base of the Coconino but thick brush covers most of the route. Rather than fight your way through the brush, it is far easier to scramble down the Talus slope found between the spring and the side trail to the dry White Creek bed below. The trail follows the creek bed until it reaches the Redwall then it moves out of the creek bed on the west side. Here the trail becomes difficult to follow as it moves through junipers on the west side of the creek bed and across three saddles to a ravine just beyond the third saddle. Descend the Redwall by going down this ravine to a ledge going southerly along the Redwall then the trail switchbacks down through the talus slopes to the creek bed below.

The trail continues to be difficult to follow as it swings to the southwest through the Tapeats then crosses Shinumo Creek to the site of Old Bass Camp. You can still identify the area where Bass and Indians before him had cultivated crops. To reach the Colorado River, the trail leaves Shinumo Creek and moves over a ridge to the south and down to the river. Across the river is old South Bass trail. Bass used cable cars and boats to cross the River at this point.

Nankoweap Trail

The Nankoweap Trail was constructed by Charles Doolittle Wolcott, a geologist who explored the Grand Canyon with Major J.W. Powell in the 1880s. Wolcott improved an old Indian trail making it suitable for horses.

As mentioned earlier, the Nankoweap/Tanner Trails connection formed a rim-to-rim route used by horsethieves and this route became known as the Horsethief Trail.

In the 1920s, man's presence on the North Rim upset the balance of nature through the protection of deer, the wanton killing of mountain lions, and the introduction of cattle and sheep. The deer overpopulated and with the addition of cattle and sheep, the area became seriously overgrazed. To alleviate the problem, an attempt was made in 1924 to herd thousands of deer from the North Rim to the South Rim via the Nankoweap Trail. Over one hundred men using various noisemakers formed a "wall" around the herd and began to move them toward the trail. When all the men finally converged on the trailhead, they were a bit chagrinned to find that they had not been successful in herding even one deer.

The Nankoweap Trailhead is located at the end of USFS Fire Road #610. The fire road begins at its intersection on the east with the paved road about 1.5 miles (2.4 kilometers) north of the North Rim Entrance Station. The distance from the trailhead to the Colorado River is about 14 miles (22.5 kilometers).

For the most part, Nankoweap trail is in bad condition with parts of the trail covered by rock slides while other parts have disappeared altogether. The latest maps of the Grand Canyon no longer show this trail and the earlier topographic maps showed the trail ending after it descended the Redwall. This is a very hot route in the summer and water is not available during any season until you reach the Colorado River. Do not attempt this trail if you are not an experienced Grand Canyon hiker.

You will find cairns marking the trailhead and again at the point where the trail descends into the Hermit Shale Formation. The trail between these two points is not too difficult to follow in spite of some brush. As the trail goes easterly toward a saddle and a small red hill near the saddle, you will find switchbacks to the north. The trail then follows the western depression of the saddle, goes southerly and switchbacks through the Esplanade. As you round the finger between Saddle Mountain and Marion Point, the trail is difficult to locate but if you look to your left and up, you should find it hidden by brush. The trail

North Bass Trail
USGS Topographic Maps
Powell Plateau Quadrangle
Havasupai Point Quadrangle

.5   0   1 Mi.

.5   0   1 Km.

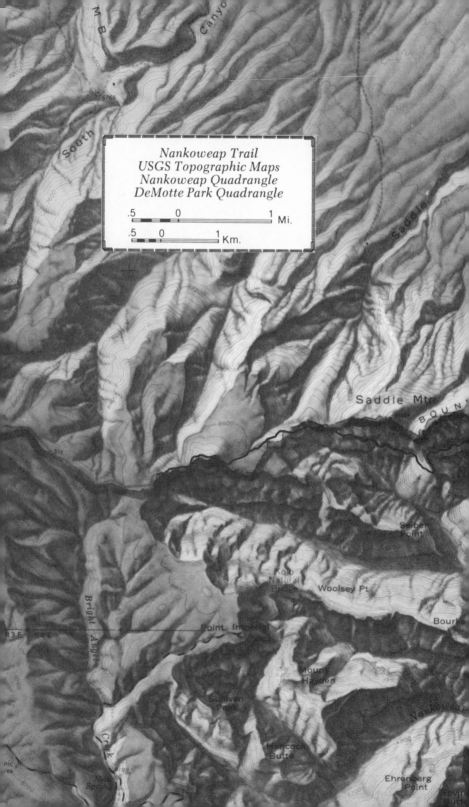

Nankoweap Trail
USGS Topographic Maps
Nankoweap Quadrangle
DeMotte Park Quadrangle

.5   0   1 Mi.

.5   0   1 Km.

follows a bench in the Supai to Tilted Mesa and the slope of the Red-wall Formation. Expect the trail to be difficult to find because of rock slides in the Supai Formation.

To descend the Redwall switchbacks, look for cairns and an arrow showing the way. When you come to a knob, go to the left of it until you reach a rock slide. At this point, you should adjust your equipment and prepare to make your way down across the slide. As you do so, try to move in the direction of a pinkish outcrop. Move across the outcrop and then down the Bright Angel slope to a drainage area serving Nankoweap Creek.

Although some hikers choose to follow the drainage area, the easier route is to follow a deer trail easterly along the shale slopes to the old horse trail emerging from the Tapeats below. Just south of the mouth of Nankoweap Creek, you will find paths leading to ancient cliff dwellings.

The North Rim

Chapter 8

Below The Rim
Day Hikes

Reservations and permits are not required to hike into the Canyon and return to the rim on the same day. If you plan a day hike keep in mind that the return trip is the most difficult part and usually requires much more time, stamina and water than the descent. Be sensible, do not overextend yourself. The accompanying table can be used as an aid for planning reasonable day hikes. The hiking times are approximate and based upon the average time required of an individual in *good* physical condition. Adjust your expected hiking time accordingly. The Park Service recommends a one-third/two-thirds split. That is, determine how many hours you want to hike and when one-third of that time has been spent, turn around and begin hiking back to the rim. There is a tendency for people to go beyond their time limit and destination because the hike into the Canyon seems relatively easy and they think the hike out can't be all that difficult. Don't be deceived. Hiking out of the Canyon is very strenuous and will test the mettle of most anyone. Details about the trails have been presented elsewhere in this book.

One Day Roundtrips

South Rim

Trails	Destination and Turnaround Point	Approximate Roundtrip Distance		Approximate Hiking Time in Hours
		Miles	Kilometers	
Bright Angel	Mile and a Half Resthouse	3	4.8	2.5-3.5
Bright Angel	Three Mile Resthouse	6	9.7	4.0-5.0
Bright Angel	Indian Gardens	9	14.5	6.0-8.0
Bright Angel and Plateau Point	Plateau Point	12	19.3	8.0-10.0
Bright Angel	Colorado River	16	25.8	12.0-14.0*
South Kaibab	Cedar Ridge	3	4.8	2.5-4.0
South Kaibab	Panorama Point	10	16.1	7.0-9.0
Hermit	Santa Maria Springs	5	8.0	5.0-6.0
Hermit and Dripping Springs	Dripping Springs	6	9.7	5.5-7.0

North Rim

Trails	Destination and Turnaround Point	Miles	Kilometers	Hours
North Kaibab	Roaring Springs	10	16.1	7.0-9.0
Lava Falls	Lava Falls (Colorado River)	1.5	2.4	6.0-7.0

*This trip should only be attempted by an experienced hiker who is in excellent physical condition. It is not recommended that this trip be attempted by anyone during the hot summer months.

Chapter 9

Havasupai Indian Reservation

A. General Information

The Havasupai Indian Reservation is located in northwestern Arizona generally west of the Grand Canyon National Park South Rim developed area. The reservation is not part of the Grand Canyon National Park and does not come under the jurisdiction of the National Park Service. All tourist facilities on the reservation including camping and hiking are managed by the Havasupai Indian tribe.

The major attraction on the reservation is Havasu Canyon (shown on some maps as Cataract Canyon). The Havasupai call this area the "Shangrila in the Grand Canyon." Havasu Creek literally springs from the canyon floor then winds through Havasu Canyon for about 10.5 miles (16.9 kilometers) until it reaches the Colorado River. Along this route are beautiful waterfalls and pools of blue-green water in terraces formed by travertine deposits. Vegetation is green and lush consisting of an interesting mixture of cacti, trees, shrubs and herbaceous plants. The area also boasts of a wide variety of birds and animals. The geological formations are quite remarkable. Throughout the Grand Canyon there is no other area that offers this rare and beautiful combination in such abundance.

The Climate

Overall, the climate in and around Havasu Canyon is moderate. The Coconino Plateau's elevations range from about 5,000 to 6,000 feet (1,524 to 1,829 meters) while Supai Village in Havasu Canyon is about 3,200 feet (975 meters) resulting in some differences in temperature between these two areas. Havasu Canyon is usually warmer than the plateau with the temperature differential much greater during the winter than the summer. Winters in Havasu Canyon are chilly but tolerable. As in other parts of the Grand Canyon, summers often bring temperatures well over 100°F (37.8°C). The most delightful times to hike into Havasu Canyon are during the spring and fall.

Precipitation in Havasu Canyon averages about 10 inches (25.40 centimeters) annually mostly in the form of rain since snow seldom reaches the canyon floor. However, expect some snow at the higher elevations during the winter. Since sudden rainstorms and flash floods do occur it is very important to check the weather forecast before starting your trip.

Average Temperatures And Precipitation

Supai Village (1979)

Month	Fahrenheit and Inches			Celsius and Centimeters		
	MAX	MIN	PRECIP	MAX	MIN	PRECIP
January	47	20	1.49	8	−7	3.78
February	54	23	.80	12	−5	2.03
March	65	32	.89	18	0	2.26
April	76	39	.20	24	4	.51
May	84	46	1.37	29	8	3.48
June	95	54	.00	35	12	.00
July	100	60	.08	38	16	.20
August	94	55	1.56	34	13	3.96
September	95	55	trace	35	13	trace
October	81	45	1.20	27	7	3.05
November	60	26	.35	16	−3	.89
December	54	23	1.25	12	−5	3.18

Source: Climatological Data, Arizona, 1979, Volume 83, Numbers 1—12, National Oceanic and Atmospheric Administration, Environmental Data and Information Service, National Climatic Center, Asheville, N.C.

B. History

Ancestors

Archaelogists and anthropologists propose that the Havasupai may be descendents of the Hokan, a group of people who crossed into the New World via the Bering Land Bridge about 30,000 years ago. The Havasupai appear to speak a language believed to be that of the Hokan group and have basically followed the Hokan's lifestyle of hunting, gathering and living in desert areas and river-bottoms.

Once in the New World the Hokan group apparently migrated southerly and settled in the Great Intermountain Basin north of the Grand Canyon area. The Hokan group pretty much had the Great Basin for themselves until about 3,000 B.C. when a new migration of people across the Bering Land Bridge created a bumping effect which ultimately moved the Hokan group from the Great Basin. This migration came from Siberia and included Athapascans who moved into the northwest areas occupied by the Shoshonean groups. The Shoshoneans then began to drift southward ahead of the Athapascans and moved into the Great Basin home of the Hokans. The Hokans eventually were displaced westward out of the Great Basin. There they began a long migration of their own.

From the Great Basin, Hokan people moved into the southern Oregon and northern California area to become the Karok, Shasta and Yana; and along the coastal valleys of California to become the Chumash, Diegueño, Pomo and Salinans. One group moved southward into Baja California, while another crossed the Colorado River near its mouth at the Gulf of California. Once on the eastern side of the Colorado River, this group of Hokans divided into two additional groups and moved in different directions. One group spread southward into Mexico, while the other followed the Gila River eastward to become the Hohokam of southcentral Arizona.

Somewhere around 600 to 800 A.D. the Hohokam were invaded by tribes from northern Mexico. To escape the invasion many of the Hohokams fled toward the Colorado River and began to follow it northward eventually reaching the plateaus of northcentral Arizona and the Grand Canyon area. Had it been possible for the Hohokam to cross the Colorado River when they first arrived in the Grand Canyon area they would have been able to return to the Great Basin, the beginning point of their long migration. Instead, they settled on the plateaus, explored the canyons and became the Cohonina, the immediate ancestors of the Havasupai. Cohonina is a derivation of

Co'onin, the Hopi name for the Havasupai. Other tribes were formed as a result of the Hohokam's trek along the Colorado River: Quechan, Cocopah, Mohave, Halchidhoma, Maricopa, Yavapai and Hualapai.

From about 800 to 1,200 A.D., the Cohonina lived on the plateau along the southern part of the Grand Canyon area through hunting, gathering and agriculture including the use of some irrigation farming. A severe drought hit the area from about 1,276 to 1,300 A.D. and the Cohonina drifted closer and closer to the San Francisco Peaks where they found themselves having to compete with other more aggressive, war-like tribes for the still life-sustaining northern slopes. According to some archaeologists and anthropologists, the Cohonina then left the plateau and returned to the spring-fed canyon areas they had discovered during their earlier migration into the area.

Unfortunately, neither the plateau nor the small low lying watered areas could alone sustain the Cohonina on a year-round basis. The versatile Cohonina adapted to their predicament by living in the watered areas during the spring and summer where they planted and harvested their crops and moved to the plateau during the winter to hunt game. One such spring-fed area was Havasu Canyon where some Cohonina already lived. They called themselves *ha vasua baaja* (People of the Blue-Green Water).

Enter The White Man

Excited by the stories of Fray Marcos, Antonio de Mendoza sent Francisco Vasquez de Coronado into Arizona in search of the seven golden cities in 1540. According to Fray Marcos, one of the cities was the Zuni pueblo, Hawikah, discovered earlier by Alvar Nunez and an African slave, Esteban. Esteban had guided Fray Marcos to Hawikah where they were imprisoned by the Zuni and Esteban was killed. Fray Marcos escaped and returned to Mexico with tales of gold and other riches he and Esteban supposedly had seen.

When Coronado and his expedition reached Hawikah they found no city of gold but established a base camp there anyway. The Zunis were eager to rid themselves of the intruders and told them stories of other cities and other places to the north where wealth was likely to be found. One of the areas described by the Zunis was the Tusayan village near the south rim of the Grand Canyon. Coronado dispatched a group of men led by Pedro de Tovar to investigate the Tusayan area. Again they found no city of gold. Instead they found several villages and farms inhabited primarily by Hopis.

Discovering the intruders, the Tusayan people took the initiative and prepared to attack. They quickly dispersed, however, when Tovar's men on horseback came galloping at them. It was a rather frightening introduction to the horse. The confrontation did not last long and peace between · Tovar and the Tusayan people was soon established.

The Tusayan people later told Tovar and his men about a wonderous canyon located just to the north. They also talked about the Co'onin (Havasupai) people who lived in parts of the Canyon. Intrigued again, Tovar sent Garcia Lopez de Cardenas and a small group of men north with a few Tusayan guides to become the first Europeans to gaze into what is now called the Grand Canyon. Although the Tusayan people were willing to lead Tovar's expedition to the edge of the Canyon, they withheld information about the routes into the Canyon. Unable to reach the Colorado River and convinced there was no way around the Canyon, Tovar and his men returned to Hawikah to rejoin the rest of Coronado's expedition.

During Coronado's expedition into the Grand Canyon area some of his horses were lost or stolen. The people living in the area, including the Havasupai, quickly recognized the value of the horse and it became one of their most important modes of transportation.

In 1768, Francisco Tomas Garcés was appointed priest at San Xavier del Bac, one of several missions founded by the legendary Jesuit priest Father Eusebio Francisco Kino. Although San Xavier was located near present-day Tucson, Father Garcés made several journeys northward in his search for new Indian tribes to convert to Christianity.

Garcés and Juan Bautista de Anzo began an expedition in October, 1775, to establish a mission and a colony in California. However, Garcés decided to leave the expedition and explore the eastern shore of the large reddish brown river he called *Rio Colorado*. Juan Bautista de Anzo's expedition went on into California and in 1776 formed a settlement which ultimately became San Francisco.

Traveling only with Indian guides, Garcés reached the western part of the Grand Canyon in the summer of 1776. Hualapai guides led him into Havasu Canyon where he became the first European to visit the Havasupai in their canyon home. He found a prosperous and friendly people who had developed a sophisticated irrigation system for farming and raised horses and cattle. Garćes was greeted warmly and remained for a five-day feast in his honor.

With the assistance of a Havasupai guide, Garcés then traveled eastward toward the mesas where the Hopis lived. He was led to another Havasupai village in Moenkopi Wash before reaching the Hopi. Apparently Garcés' Havasupai guide's brother was the leader of this small group (about 30) of Havasupai and they stopped to visit for awhile. Garcés found the Hopi much less friendly and hospitable then the Havasupai and he soon left to return to *Rio Jabesua* (Havasu

Creek). Upon his return, the Havasupai apparently celebrated with a six-day feast.

Later, Garcés left the Grand Canyon area following a trail used by Havasupai traders from Havasu Canyon to the Mohave. After returning to San Xavier, Garcés set out again and established a mission on the lower Gila River. In 1781 he was killed at his mission by the Mohave.

In the 1850s the Havasupai territory was being explored and surveyed for a transcontinental railroad. One expedition was led by Lorenzo Sitgreaves in 1851 and another by Joseph Christmas Ives in 1858. The Sitgreaves expedition stayed primarily on the plateau while the Ives expedition attempted, in vain, to navigate the Colorado River in a small steamboat. In 1866, the Atlantic & Pacific Railroad received from the U.S. Congress a right of way for their proposed through Oklahoma, New Mexico and Arizona. Included in this right of way was an indemnity grant consisting of the odd sections of land 40 miles (64 kilometers) outwards from the right of way. In some areas, such as the Havasupai territory, the railroad was indemnified beyond the forty-mile limit. These indemnified lands became part of a bitter dispute between the Havasupai and the Federal Government for many years.

By the 1870s, miners were being drawn to the Grand Canyon area by dreams of vast quantities of gold, silver, copper and other minerals. The miners often entered the Grand Canyon following Indian trails. More often than not, prospectors found only small but hardly profitable deposits of minerals.

Some silver was discovered in Havasu Canyon by Charles Spencer in 1873, while W.C. Beckman and H.J. Young established a lead-silver operation in 1879—80 below what is now called Havasu Falls.

In 1880, a former sailor-turned-prospector named James Mooney and a group of friends entered Havasu Canyon hoping to discover rich mineral deposits. When they reached the top of the largest falls, called the *Mother of Waters* by the Havasupai, they could find no route to the bottom except by descending the sheer cliff walls. Mooney was the first to try and as his companions lowered him over the side of the cliff by rope, they found that the rope was not long enough to reach the bottom. Mooney was unable to climb the rope back to the top and eventually lost his grip before his companions could bring him back to safety. He fell to his death on the rocks at the base of the falls.

Some say that Mooney's friends returned a little less than a year later and finally made their way down the cliff to where Mooney fell. To their surprise they found Mooney's body encased in a travertine formation created from the waterfall's spray. They buried him on an island below the waterfall. The waterfall has been known as Mooney Falls ever since.

Mooney Falls

During the late 1800s and early 1900s, miners searched for minerals throughout the Havasupai area. Most of the major activity took place in Carbonate Canyon near Havasu Falls, but tunnels and other evidence of mining activity can be found all along Havasu Creek from Havasu Falls to the Colorado River. Miners were also responsible for cutting the route through the travertine formation at Mooney Falls.

Mineral deposits were not rich and getting ore out of the Canyon to market proved to be a very difficult and expensive task. Mining activity began to wane until the early 1930s when a trail past Havasu Falls was constructed with the help of the Civilian Conservation Corps. About this time W.I. Johnson, who owned Arizona Lead & Zinc Company, sold his mining claims near Havasu Falls to E.F. Schoeny. The mine, with low productivity and profitability, remained essentially closed until World War II when the demand for lead increased dramatically. During the war the mine was reopened, but soon after the war mining operations no longer were profitable and the mine was again closed. Over the years Johnson and Schoeny had constructed cabins complete with running water and electricity in the area and after the war the Havasupai entered into an agreement with Schoeny to rent the cabins to campers and other visitors.

In 1957, the National Park Service acquired the mining claims from Schoeny. Eventually the cabins were destroyed and the area was transformed into a public campground operated as part of the Grand Canyon National Park until 1975. This area was the site of ancient Havasupai cremation and burial grounds.

The Tale Of Two Reservations

In the 1870s the Havasupai were already feeling the effects of the newly arriving white man's interest in the plateau land for grazing and the canyon lands for mining. The Havasupai often found themselves shut-out of areas they had occupied for centuries. By 1880, John C. Fremont, Governor of Arizona Territory, decided to take action in order to protect the white man's growing interest in the area and to avoid possible serious confrontations between the Havasupai and the ranchers and miners. He requested that the federal government establish a Havasupai Reservation. Governor Fremont recommended an area 2 miles (3.2 kilometers) wide and 12 miles (19.3 kilometers) long along Havasu Creek. The beginning point was to be 2 miles (3.2 kilometers) below Mooney Falls and ending some 12 miles (19.3 kilometers) upstream. President Rutherford B. Hayes responded quickly and on June 8, 1880 he issued an Executive Order establishing a reservation encompassing an area along Havasu Creek 12 miles (19.3 kilometers) long and 2.5 miles (4.0 kilometers) on each side of the

Creek, an area 3 miles (4.8 kilometers) wider than suggested by Governor Fremont. The President also ordered the U.S. Army Corps of Engineers to survey the area and mark the boundaries.

When the surveying party arrived in the summer of 1881 to mark the boundaries of the newly created reservation, they found their task next to impossible. The complex topography of the area did not fit at all well with the simply stated description presented in the Executive Order. Two and-one-half miles (4.0 kilometers) on each side of Havasu Creek placed the east-west boundaries on top of the presumably inaccessible mesas. Further, even if markers could be placed on the mesas, they could not be seen from the bottom of the canyon. This made it impossible for the surveying party to connect the boundaries.

Lt. Carl F. Palfrey, who was conducting the survey, became very frustrated at his task and finally asked the Havasupai Chief, Navajo, to assist in marking the land that Chief Navajo wanted to be included in the reservation. The boundaries selected by Lt. Palfrey and Chief Navajo included only the bottom land of Havasu Canyon along Havasu Creek beginning at the crest of Mooney Falls and extending upstream about 6.5 miles (10.5 kilometers), an area of 518.6 acres (209.9 hectares). The area selected was much smaller than dictated in the Executive Order and did not include any of the aboriginal plateau lands. The smaller Havasupai Reservation was made official on March 31, 1882, by President Chester A. Arthur.

Two explanations are given for Chief Navajo's selection of such a small reservation. The first involves his desire to occupy only those lands he felt he could defend adequately. The second was a need to cooperate because he feared any opposition would result in his people being removed from the land altogether and sent to a foreign land to die. His fear of removal was justified because a few years earlier (1874) the Hualapais were removed from their land and moved south to the Colorado River Reservation near present-day Ehrenburg where many died of starvation and disease. In 1875 the surviving Hualapais simply walked away from the reservation and returned to their traditional lands. Indeed, the Colorado River Reservation was established in 1865 for the expressed purpose of confining all of Arizona's Indian tribes there.

At the time the reservation was being established, the Havasupai were given assurances by various government officials that they could continue to use the plateau land as they had for centuries. But when they tried, more often than not, they encountered white settlers who threatened to kill them. Ranchers soon claimed the ancient water tanks built by the Havasupai and prevented the Havasupai from using them. Even when the Hualapai Reservation was established in 1883 it included some traditional Havasupai plateau land.

By 1886, the Atlantic & Pacific Railroad had still failed to meet its obligation to complete a railroad line across Oklahoma, New Mexico and Arizona so the U.S. Congress revoked the indemnity grant for a right of way given to A & P in 1866. These odd sections of land 40 miles (64 kilometers) outward from the right of way were then placed in the public domain. Some of these lands were traditional Havasupai plateau land. Although efforts were made by Lt. Col. G.N. Brayton and General Nelson Miles in 1888 to expand the Havasupai Reservation to include some of these newly released plateau lands, the efforts failed and more white settlers moved into the area.

To make matters worse for the Havasupai, President Benjamin Harrison signed an Executive Order in 1893 creating the Grand Cañon Forest Reserve. The Reserve contained Havasupai plateau lands and completely surrounded the Havasupai Reservation. In 1896, the Superintendent of the Havasupai Reservation, Henry P. Ewing, requested that the Havasupai Reservation be expanded to include some of the newly created Grand Cañon Forest Reserve. His request was denied as the government not only did not plan to relinquish any of the Reserve but was also again considering moving the Havasupai to the Colorado River Reservation. This sparked several angry exchanges between Superintendent Ewing and various federal agencies over the rights of the Havasupai to use Reserve land and the government's intention to remove them from their home. Things continued to go badly for the Havasupai with confrontations on the plateau becoming increasingly more hostile and dangerous. In 1898, the Forestry Department and the Grand Cañon Forest Reserve Superintendent, W.P. Herman, took a strong stand and recommended to the Office of Indian Affairs that the Havasupai not be allowed to use any of the Reserve land for any purpose. The Office of Indian Affairs accepted this recommendation and instructed Superintendent Ewing to confine the Havasupai to the reservation, effectively depriving them of their winter range and their aboriginal lands.

Superintendent Ewing resisted and continued to champion the Havasupai's cause and in 1900 he again requested an expanded reservation. The request was denied in 1901 and the government finally won the battle with Superintendent Ewing in 1902 when he was summarily removed from office.

In 1908, the Grand Cañon Forest Reserve was completely reorganized and an effort again was made to set aside some of the plateau for an expanded Havasupai Reservation. As in the past, the effort failed but the Havasupai were granted permission to use about 100,000 acres (40,469 hectares) of plateau land for grazing purposes.

For the next eight years the Havasupai attempted to have this permit land and other plateau land added to their reservation. However, the various government agencies became less and less interested because now there was a growing interest instead in creating a national park in the area. Indeed, the National Park Service Act was passed in 1916 and on February 26, 1919, the Grand Canyon National Park was established through the passage of Senate Bill 8250 introduced about a year earlier by Senator Henry Ashurst and Representative Carl Hayden, both from Arizona. The bill creating the Park allowed for the use of land within the Park by the Havasupai, but only by permit issued by the Secretary of Interior and only for agricultural purposes.

By the 1930s all attempts to return plateau land to the Havasupai had failed and in 1932 President Herbert Hoover created a Grand Canyon National Monument from the Atlantic & Pacific lands located in the western part of traditional Havasupai plateau land. For the next sixteen years one attempt after another to restore various plateau lands either from the Forest Service or the National Park Service was turned away even when the Havasupai found supporters for their cause from legislators or from within various governmental agencies.

In order to settle land claims made by the various American Indian tribes against the U.S. Government, Congress created the Indian Claims Commission in 1946. The Indians had a maximum of five years to file suit in order to receive payment for land taken from them. The Havasupai were much less interested in the money than in having their land returned to them and were reluctant to file a suit for that reason. However, the Bureau of Indian Affairs convinced the Havasupai to file suit in 1951 mainly because there seemed to be little chance that any land was going to be returned to Indian tribes and if the Havasupai did not sue they would gain nothing.

Seventeen years later (1968), the Indian Claims Commission offered a settlement of the Havasupai suit. The Havasupai were offered $1,240,000 for being deprived of 2,257,728 acres (913,670 hectares) or about 55¢ per acre (.4 hectare) of prime Grand Canyon land! Now the Havasupai were in a dilemma because they had recently found strong support from Arizona Congressman John Rhoades and Sam Steiger to have about 173,000 acres (70,011 hectares) of plateau land contained in the Kaibab National Forest and the Grand Canyon National Park returned to them. They saw accepting the monetary settlement as the end of their efforts to get their land back. They still wanted their land, not the money. However, the tribal claims lawyer, Royal D. Marks, and the Bureau of Indian Affairs advised that accepting the settlement did not mean the Havasupai could not attempt to regain their land through congressional action. The Havasupai voted to accept the settlement in 1969. Within two years a new master plan for an expanded Grand Canyon National Park was being developed which encompassed all of the previous Havasupai permit lands. Their fears were being realized: the Havasupai would get the money and they would lose their aboriginal home.

In 1971, the Havasupai objected strongly to the master plan and although the Park Service seemed willing to return some land to them, the Forest Service took a firm stand. Of particular concern to the Havasupai were the Hualapai Hilltop area and the Pasture Wash grazing land. Some negotiations occurred for a couple of years but essentially nothing was settled. At about this time Arizona Senator Barry Goldwater was preparing to introduce Senate Bill 1296 to officially expand the Grand Canyon National Park. The Havasupai presented their case to Senator Goldwater and found a supporter. He included the Havasupai's claim to certain plateau lands as part of the bill. A similar House version was introduced by Arizona Congressman Morris K. Udall. The introduction of these bills with provisions for returning Grand Canyon area land to the Havasupai touched off a bitter fight among environmentalist groups, the Bureau of Indian Affairs, the National Park Service, the National Forest Service, the Office of Management and Budget, the U.S. Congress, the White House and the Havasupai Tribe which lasted for nearly three years. Finally on January 3, 1975, President Gerald Ford signed into law P.L. 93-620 which approved the expansion of the Grand Canyon National Park and the return of the largest amount of aboriginal land to one American Indian tribe in history. The Havasupai Indian Reservation now contains about 185,000 acres (74,867 hectares) plus an adjoining 95,000 acres (38,445 hectares) of permanent land use.

How To Get There

Although there are several routes into Havasu Canyon, only the one via Hualapai Hilltop and the Hualapai Trail is maintained by the Havasupai for use by visitors. The use of all other routes is discouraged by the Havasupai in order to regulate the number of visitors and protect the integrity of the environment and their ancestral home. Most of the other routes are primitive and potentially dangerous.

To reach Hualapai Hilltop and the Hualapai Trailhead, follow U.S. Route 66 toward Peach Springs, Arizona. Approximately 7 miles (11 kilometers) east of Peach Springs and 33 miles (53 kilometers) west of Seligman you will find a paved road leading toward the northeast. This road winds across the Coconino Plateau for approximately 63 miles (101 kilometers) until it ends at Hualapai Hilltop. This route across the Coconino Plateau has been gradually improved over the past several years and is now a well-maintained road of which all but the last few miles are paved. Since no services of any kind are available once you leave Route 66, take care to have enough fuel, water and food for the roundtrip.

Hualapai Hilltop consists of a large lighted parking lot, a couple of toilets, a few picnic tables, a staging area for pack animals and the trailhead. No water is available on the Hilltop and camping involves finding a spot large and flat enough to lie down. Overlooking Hualapai Canyon, the Hilltop provides an excellent view of the valley below and the first few miles of the trail.

C. Accommodations Outside
The Havasupai Reservation

There are three areas near the access road to Hualapai Hilltop on U.S. Route 66 where supplies, services, food, lodging and/or camping are available.

Grand Canyon Caverns

The area nearest to the access road is a privately owned enterprise called Grand Canyon Caverns, formerly Dinosaur Caverns. Located approximately 3 miles (5 kilometers) east of the access road, the Grand Canyon Caverns offers camping, a motel with swimming pool, a restaurant, a cocktail lounge, and a service station. Also available is a 4,200 feet (1,280 meters) surfaced airstrip with tiedowns and a taxi strip to the motel. For more detailed information and reservations contact:

Caverns Inn
Highway 66
Dinosaur City, Arizona
Telephone: Place call through the Prescott, AZ operator.

Seligman, Arizona

Located approximately 33 miles (53 kilometers) east of the access road, this small town offers the usual services for the traveler. For lodging contact:

Aztec Motel	Deluxe Motel	Romney Motel
(602) 422-3272	(602) 422-3244	(602) 422-3294
Bil-Mar-Den	Navajo Motel	Supai Motel
(602) 422-3470	(602) 422-3312	(602) 422-3663
Canyon Shadows Motel		
(602) 422-3255		

For camping contact:

KOA Campgrounds	Northern Arizona Campground
(602) 422-3358	(602) 422-3549

Peach Springs—Truxton, Arizona Area

The nearest area for services to the west of the access road is the Peach Springs—Truxton area, approximately 7 miles (11 kilometers). Peach Springs is located on the Hualapai (not Havasupai) Reservation. For lodging contact:

> Frontier Motel and Cafe
> (602) 769-2238

D. Accommodations In Havasu Canyon

Supai Village

Supai Village, located in Havasu Canyon, has overnight accommodations at the Schoolhouse Canyon Lodge and the Supai Lodge. Each Lodge has a few rooms with a shared kitchen complete with all the necessary cooking and eating implements. Reservations are required. Normally, reservations need to be made at least four to eight weeks in advance.

The Havasupai Tribe operates a small general store and a cafe in Supai Village. Some groceries and other supplies may be purchased at the general store while the cafe offers breakfast, sandwiches and related fare. Special treats are Indian Fry Bread and homemade desserts.

Supai Village also has the only remaining post office in the United States which receives and transports mail by animal pack train.

Camping

Overnight camping is permitted only in designated tribal campgrounds. Water, picnic tables and toilets are available at these sites. Major campgrounds are located near Navajo Falls and between Havasu and Mooney Falls. No open fires are allowed so it is necessary to bring your own source of heat for cooking. Pets are not allowed. Campsites are limited and reservations for camping are required. Normally, reservations should be made at least four to twelve weeks in advance. Summer months and weekends throughout the year are the most difficult times to obtain reservations unless you do so well in advance. Hikers are required to pay an entrance fee as well as a per night camping fee.

Saddle And Pack Horses

Saddle and/or pack horses are available for one-way or round trips between Hualapai Hilltop and Supai Village or the campgrounds. Advance reservations and a deposit are usually required.

Reservations For Visitor Services

The Havasupai Tribe manages all visitor services including lodges, camping and horses. For reservations and detailed information contact: *(start Jan. 2nd)* *called in May / 8 ♦: filled up thru part of July*

> Havasupai Tourist Enterprise
> Supai, Arizona 86435
> Telephone: (602) 448-2121

♦ 8 person entrance fee
♦ 7 day per person/night to camp.
(most people stay 2-3 days no one 7 day)

Hualapai Trail

The approximate distances from Hualapai Hilltop to various points in Havasu Canyon via the Hualapai Trail are:

Destination	Miles	Kilometers
Havasu Creek	6.5	10.5
Supai Village	8.0	12.9
Navajo Falls and Campground	9.5	15.3
Havasu Falls and Campground	10.0	16.1
Mooney Falls	11.0	17.7
Beaver Falls	12.0	19.3
Colorado River	17.0	27.4

The trail begins at Hualapai Hilltop with a series of steep switchbacks, then descends more gradually across the valley until it drops into a normally dry creek bed. The trail follows the creek bed to the northeast through Hualapai Canyon. Water can sometimes be found on the trail a short distance beyond the point where the trail meets the creek bed. Look for a metal watering trough for animals on the west side of the trail. Located above the trough on a large boulder is a concrete and stone structure with a metal faucet. Appropriately, a smiling face adorns this structure. This source of water is unreliable, however.

As the trail winds in and out of the creek bed it passes through increasingly narrow passages. At times you will pass between towering canyon walls and beneath incredible overhangs carved out by centuries of rushing waters. Just when you begin to feel that you have lost your way and have somehow stumbled into Dante's Inferno, the canyon begins to widen and soon you find yourself in the midst of tall cotton-

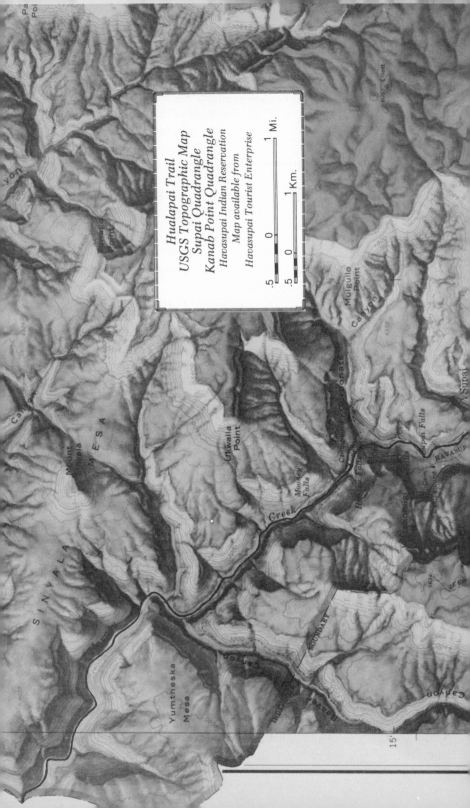

Hualapai Trail
USGS Topographic Map
Supai Quadrangle
Kanab Point Quadrangle
Havasupai Indian Reservation
Map available from
Havasupai Tourist Enterprise

.5   0   1 Mi.

.5   0   1 Km.

woods and willows. You have arrived at the first dependable water source. Havasu Springs, the beginning of Havasu Creek.

Havasu Springs is the result of the drainage of over 3,000 square miles (7,770 square kilometers) of the Coconino Plateau. Formed primarily of porous limestone, the plateau provides little resistance to rainwater which easily seeps down and through it. The water then travels underground until it reaches a point in Havasu Canyon where the water-bearing stratum is finally exposed. It is at this point where the water escapes its subterranean confinement and begins an above-ground 10 mile (16.1 kilometers) trip to the Colorado River.

The trail generally follows the creek downstream for about 1 mile (1.6 kilometers) and then swings away from the creek toward Supai Village. Along the way you will notice an irrigation system channeling water from Havasu Creek to the outlying Havasupai farms. This system represents modern improvements on an irrigation network used for centuries by the Havasupai.

As the trail approaches Supai Village it climbs somewhat, providing a very nice view of the farms and the canyon walls. Looking across the canyon you will see two pillar-like rock formations perched on top of the canyon walls. These formations are male and female deities called *Wigeleeva*. They are the guardians of the Havasupai people and their crops. An ancient Havasupai story states that the *Wigeleeva* protect the Havasupai people from harm and cause their gardens to be bountiful; and, if the *Wigeleeva* should ever fall, the village and the Havasupai people will be destroyed.

The trail continues a short distance through outlying farms and homesites until it reaches Supai Village, the center of Havasupai social, business and educational activities. All visitors must check in at the Tourist Office in Supai Village. If you have reservations for camping, you will pay your fees here and be assigned to a campground.

Navajo Falls and Navajo Campground are about 1.5 miles (2.4 kilometers) from Supai Village while Havasu Falls and Havasu Campground are about 2 miles (3.2 kilometers) from Supai Village. Of course, the trail to the falls is well marked and easy to follow.

At Havasu Falls, sometimes called Bridal Veil Falls for reasons that will become obvious to you, you will approach the falls from the top. It is here that you will be treated to your first really good view of the beautiful deep blue and blue-green pools at the base of the falls. Looking beyond Havasu Falls to the northeast you will see Carbonate Canyon, the site of mining activity in the late 1800s and early 1900s. The trail drops along the side of the falls and moves into the campgrounds near the creek. No camping is permitted at the base of the falls but swimming is allowed.

Mooney Falls is about 1 miles (1.6 kilometers) downstream from

Havasu Falls. At about 200 feet (61 meters), Mooney Falls is the highest of the Havasu Canyon Falls. To reach the base of the falls, you must descend a sheer cliff wall through two small tunnels. At one point there are very steep footholds in the rock and a chain to hold on to. No camping is permitted below Mooney Falls but, again, swimming is allowed.

Hiking below Mooney Falls toward Beaver Falls (about 1 mile; 1.6 kilometers) and the Colorado River (about 5 miles; 8.1 kilometers) requires that you cross the creek several times so prepare yourself and your gear accordingly. A round trip from the campgrounds to the Colorado River can easily consume most of a day.

Wigleeva

Trail into Hualapai Canyon

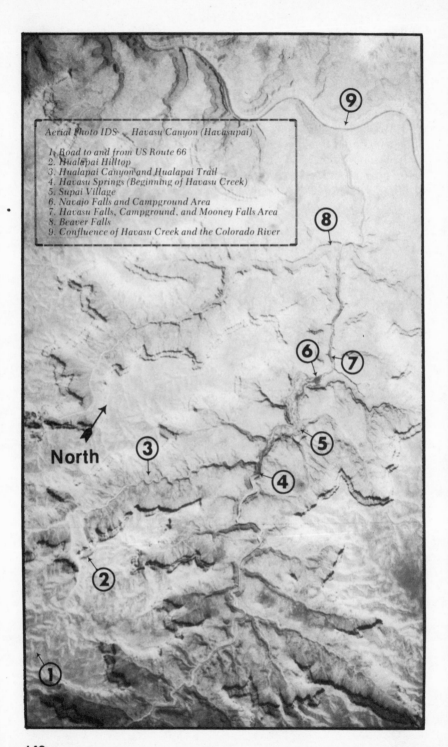

Aerial Photo IDS — Havasu Canyon (Havasupai)

1. Road to and from US Route 66
2. Hualapai Hilltop
3. Hualapai Canyon and Hualapai Trail
4. Havasu Springs (Beginning of Havasu Creek)
5. Supai Village
6. Navajo Falls and Campground Area
7. Havasu Falls, Campground, and Mooney Falls Area
8. Beaver Falls
9. Confluence of Havasu Creek and the Colorado River

North

Recommended Reading

Hiking And Backpacking

Berkowitz, Alan, *Guide to the Bright Angel Trail*, Grand Canyon Natural History Association, Arizona.

Butchart, Harvey, *Grand Canyon Treks*, La Siesta Press, Glendale, California, 1970.

Butchart, Harvey, *Grand Canyon Treks II*, La Siesta Press, Glendale, California, 1975.

Fear, Gene, *Surviving the Unexpected Wilderness Emergency*, Survival Education Association, Tacoma, Washington, 1975.

Fletcher, Colin, *The Man Who Walked Through Time*, Alfred A. Knopf, New York, 1967.

Hiking the Inner Canyon: A Guide, Grand Canyon Natural History Association, Arizona. (Compiled by the Backcountry Reservations Office and Bob Butterfield, Division of Interpretation.)

Kjellstrom, Bjorn, *Be Expert With Map & Compass, The Orienteering Handbook*, Charles Scribner's Sons, New York, 1976.

Manning, Harvey, *Backpacking: One Step at a Time*, Vintage Books, New York, 1980.

History And General

Babbitt, Bruce, *Grand Canyon An Anthology*, Northland Press, Flagstaff, Arizona, 1978.

Beal, Merrill D., *Grand Canyon, The Story Behind the Scenery*, K C Publications, Las Vegas, Nevada, 1978.

Hughes, J. Donald, *In The House of Stone and Light*, Grand Canyon Natural History Association, Arizona, 1978.

James, George Wharton, *In and Around the Grand Canyon*, Little, Brown & Co., Boston, 1900.

James, George Wharton, *The Grand Canyon of Arizona*, Little, Brown & Co., Boston, 1910.

Kolb, Ellsworth L., *Through the Grand Canyon from Wyoming to Mexico*, The MacMillan Company, New York, 1969.

Krutch, Joseph Wood, *Grand Canyon Today and All Its Yesterdays*, William Morrow & Co., New York, 1958.

Leydet, Francois, *Time and the River Flowing: Grand Canyon*, Sierra Club, San Francisco, 1964.

Nash, Roderick, (Ed.), *Grand Canyon of the Living Colorado*, Sierra Club, San Francisco, 1970.

National Parkways, A Photographic and Comprehensive Guide to Grand Canyon National Park, World-wide Research and Publishing Company, Casper, Wyoming, 1977.

Powell, John Wesley, *Exploration of the Colorado River of the West and Its Tributaries*, Government Printing Office, Washington, D.C., 1875.

Sutton, Ann and Sutton, Myron, *The Wilderness World of the Grand Canyon*, J.P. Lippincott, New York, 1970.

Wallace, Robert, *The Grand Canyon*, Time-Life Books, New York, 1972.

Watkins, T.H., (Ed.), *The Grand Colorado*, American West Publishing Co., Palo Alto, California, 1969.

Geology

Breed, William J., and Roat, Evelyn C., (Eds), *Geology of the Grand Canyon*, Museum of Northern Arizona and Grand Canyon Natural History Association, Flagstaff, Arizona, 1974.

U.S. Department of the Interior Geological Survey, *Plan and Profile of Colorado River from Lees Ferry, Arizona, to Black Canyon, Arizona-Nevada, and Virgin River, Nevada*, Government Printing Office, Washington, D.C., 1924.

Havasupai

Coues, Elliott, (Trans. and Ed.), *On the Trail of a Spanish Pioneer; The Diary and Itinerary of Francisco Garcès*, F.P. Harper, New York, 1900.

Cushing, Frank H., "The Nation of the Willows", *Atlantic Monthly*, 50, Sept. and Oct. 1882 (Also available in book form from Northland Press, Flagstaff, Arizona).

Dobyns, Henry F., and Euler, Robert C., *The Havasupai People*, Indian Tribal Series, Phoenix, Arizona, 1971.

Dobyns, Henry F., and Euler, Robert C., *Wauba Yuma's People*, Prescott College Press, Prescott, Arizona, 1970.

Ellis, Richard N., (Ed.), *The Western American Indian: Case Studies in Tribal History*, University of Nebraska Press, Lincoln, Nebraska, 1972.

Hirst, Stephen, *Life in a Narrow Place*, David McKay Company, New York, 1976.

Iliff, Flora Gregg, *People of the Blue Water*, Harper & Brothers, New York, 1954.

James, George Wharton, *Havasupai Indians*, Little, Brown and Co., 1907.

Johnston, Jay, "Indian Shangri-La of the Grand Canyon," *National Geographic*, March, 1970.

Josephy, Alvin M., Jr., *The Indian Heritage of America*, Alfred A. Knopf, New York, 1968.

Kroeber, Alfred Louis, (Ed.), *Walapai Ethnography*, Memoirs of the American Anthropological Association, Number 42, 1935.

Schroeder, Albert L., "A Brief History of the Havasupai," *Plateau*, 25:4, 1952. (Museum of Northern Arizona, Flagstaff, Arizona.)

Schwartz, Douglas W., "Prehistoric Man in the Grand Canyon," *Scientific American*, 198:8-11, 1958.

Schwartz, Douglas W., "The Havasupai 600 A.D.—1500 A.D.: A Short Cultural History," *Plateau*, 28:4, 1956. (Museum of Northern Arizona, Flagstaff, Arizona.)

Smithson, Carma Lee, and Euler, Robert C., *Havasupai Religion and Mythology*, University of Utah Anthropological Papers, Number 68, April 1964.

Spier, Leslie, "Havasupai Ethnography," *Anthropological Papers of the American Museum of Natural History*, New York, 29, Part 3, 1928.

Wampler, Joseph, *Havasu Canyon: Gem of the Grand Canyon*, Howell-North Press, Berkeley, California, 1959.

Wilder, Carleton S., "Archaeological Survey of the Great Thumb Area, Grand Canyon National Park," *Plateau*, 17:2, 1944. (Museum of Northern Arizona, Flagstaff, Arizona.)

AZTEX Corporation, — Information:

This book is part of a continuing project. Please advise us of any additions or corrections which you come across in reading this volume. Any information, no matter how obscure or seemingly unimportant, is welcomed. In sending information, please make reference to the title and author and mail to: *Editor, AZTEX Corporation, P O Box 50046, Tucson, Arizona 85703.*